Bibliographic information published by the German National Library:

The German National Library lists this publication in the National Bibliography; detailed bibliographic data are available on the Internet at http://dnb.dnb.de .

Imprint:

Copyright © 2016 GRIN Verlag, Open Publishing GmbH
Print and binding: Books on Demand GmbH, Norderstedt Germany
ISBN: 9783668330115

This book at GRIN:

http://www.grin.com/en/e-book/342425/the-hit-and-significance-of-augmented-reality-application-and-treatments

Avery Jerome Agboro

The hit and significance of augmented reality. Application and treatments in tertiary education

A case study of Mauritius

GRIN Publishing

GRIN - Your knowledge has value

Since its foundation in 1998, GRIN has specialized in publishing academic texts by students, college teachers and other academics as e-book and printed book. The website www.grin.com is an ideal platform for presenting term papers, final papers, scientific essays, dissertations and specialist books.

Visit us on the internet:

http://www.grin.com/

http://www.facebook.com/grincom

http://www.twitter.com/grin_com

THE HIT AND SIGNIFICANCE OF AUGMENTED REALITY.

Application and treatments in Tertiary Education:

A CASE STUDY OF MAURITIUS.

Author: Agboro Avery Jerome.

ADSE: *Advanced Diploma in Software Engineering,* **BSC** *Information technology & Business Information System,* **MBA** *International Business.*

A Freelance Journal

Research period: 10/01/16 – 10/11/2016

"A scientific research that convers the significance of ARI"

ABSTRACT

The related study researched the effect of Augmented Reality (AR) on understudies' learning inside a tertiary training setting. Unequivocally, it measured learning upgrade levels, inspiration and the apparent acknowledgment of the innovation as members occupied with a lesson identifying with the human mind life systems. An aggregate of 80 exploration members from the Middlesex University Mauritius Branch Campus participated in the study. They were selected from an assortment of offices and relegated arbitrarily in a split 40:40 proportion to 2 bunches: (1) Augmented Reality Instruction (ARI); and (2) Traditional Instruction (TI). In light of their allotted bunches, members were either treated to Augmented Reality based directions or Traditional 2D guidelines. Toward the end of the lesson, members from both gatherings were required to take a post-test taking into account what they had learnt. Moreover, members that participated in the Augmented Reality Instruction treatment, were additionally required to take a Technology Acceptance test. Investigation of results got from the post-tests of both ARI and TI treatment bunches, highlighted a solid huge distinction in learning picks up. Furthermore, the Technology Acceptance test taken by the ARI bunch likewise demonstrated that the utilization of AR, positively affected understudies' inspiration to learn, furthermore reflected as the fundamental purpose behind their acknowledgment of the innovation.

TABLE OF CONTENTS

CHAPTER 1:
INTRODUCTION

Throughout the years, innovative progressions have been known not new and one of a kind open doors for various fields of work and training has been no exemption. For instance, through many years of persistent exploration, it has been set up that the utilization of processing innovations inside classroom settings, can improve both educating and learning exercises (**Strijbos, 2011; Karvounidis et al., 2014**). This is in contrast with settings lacking such guides. Increased Reality (AR), an idea which gives space for the consistent coordination of virtual and physical areas, postures as one of the most recent pertinent innovative interests sought after. This innovation, which previously, has generally been out of sight, now introduces a one of a kind door towards augmenting the range of human abilities crosswise over both the instructive and different trains alike (**Nicholson, 2013**). From an instructive point of view, AR gives space for the comprehension of many-sided marvels through the procurement of visual and particularly intuitive learning encounters (**Wang, 2012**). It consolidates both virtual and genuine data with an end goal to better convey issues, standards or presentation objects of conceptual nature to learners (**Wang, 2012; Bloxham, 2014**). Using AR, creators are given the way to superimpose graphical representations of virtual nature over genuine ecological items, furnishing clients with a way to interface and physically control the graphical substance. The consequence of this combination exhibits an all the more convincing presentation of both spatial and transient related ideas, combined with the relevant connections between the virtual and genuine articles. The innovation is as of now demonstrating guarantee in supporting understudy learning upgrades in respect to customary methods of instructing inside preschool and grade school settings (**Duenser and Hornecker, 2007; Dunleavy, Dede, and Mitchell, 2008; Klopfer and Squire, 2008; Chang, Morreale and Medicherla, 2010**). That being said, more research in accordance with giving solid confirmation on the impacts of its execution from tertiary level points of view is still in need towards building up the innovation's predominance.

1.1 Research questions and study objectives.

The present concentrate in this way, tries to analyse the impacts of an AR instructional treatment to the general customary method of educating on tertiary level understudies in Mauritius. An AR application will be produced with the goal to examine the outcomes got from its execution. The exploration's prime goals being to evaluate the level of information maintenance, motivational impact and acknowledgment from the use of the innovation inside a tertiary instruction class setting. Research inquiries to guide this request are as per the following:

1.   Can learning encouraged by AR upgrade understudy getting a handle on force?

2.   Does AR based learning grow the capacity to focus and engagement of understudies?

3.   Can AR be acknowledged as a suitable mentoring instrument inside tertiary Institutions?

1.2 Overview

Keeping in mind the end goal to accomplish the destinations of the study, this exposition has been separated into 9 sections: an audit of writing, configuration, usage, approach, information investigation and results, talk, conclusion, references and the supplement. The survey of writing will begin off by clarifying the idea of expanded reality from the point of view of various specialists and scholastics. It will then progress into highlighting logical uses of its execution in various fields of tries and current headways inside the instructive segment. The part will be finished by focusing on the requirement for the study and the proposed inquiries to be replied. The outline area will transfer points of interest in light of programming and equipment necessities, legitimization of their decisions, expected capacities, and objectives of the AR application to be planned. In the execution segment, contemplations and definite strides completed to accomplish the last item would be introduced. Inside the system segment, the decision of connected procedure will be highlighted combined with a depiction of the members and test populace determination. Legitimization of instruments utilized and information gathering systems will likewise be transferred in this area. Tailing this, an examination of the information gathered and last results of the activity will be handed-off inside the information investigation and results and area. The exchange area will begin by repeating the examination inquiries and objectives, trailed by a compelling synopsis of all discoveries. This area will advance intend to put the related discoveries into setting through a point by point basic examination. To round off, the conclusion segment will give last declarations on the exploration, its discoveries and suggestions. Experienced requirements will likewise be handed-off now taking after by recommendations for future works. All references to outside sourced materials will be incorporated into references area and the index segment will contain codes composed and different materials not specifically vital to the principle body of the paper.

CHAPTER 2:
RESEARCH BACKGROUND

This section highlights the idea driving Augmented Reality and its definition from the viewpoints of different specialists. It likewise reveals some insight into commendable usage of AR in different fields, strikingly in the field of instruction and indisputably focuses on the targets and expectations of the study.

2.1 Concept and definitions

Increased Reality (AR) is an idea that has been in presence for more than 50 years (Johnson et al., 2011), yet has been increasing quite a bit of its ubiquity as of late. This can be ascribed to the rise of a more extensive scope of open supporting advances which are less expensive, quicker, more versatile, shrewder and simple to utilize. Distinctive specialists throughout the years have introduced definitions with an end goal to clarify this interesting idea; some of which are exhibited in the table beneath.

AR definitions from scientists throughout the years according to scholars and other academic like minds. **Azuma (1997)** A mechanical adjustment from Virtual Reality that means to supplement reality by bringing virtual items into it. **Hollerer and Feiner (2004)** Technologies that union both PC outlined and genuine articles in an adjusted manner, altogether inside a physical situation and in real time. **Ludwig and Reimann (2005)** A method of human-based PC cooperation (HCI) that presents objects of virtual nature, anticipated by camcorders in real time, to genuine discernment. **Zhou, Duh and Billinghurst (2008)** A mechanical means by which PC composed symbolism of virtual nature are anticipated to precisely overlay certifiable articles in genuine time. **El Sayed, Zayed, and Sharawy (2011)** A apparatus that permits the presentation of extra data in genuine situations with the guide of virtual articles. **Chen and Tsai (2012)** A innovation that shows the capacity to collaborate with for all intents and purposes displayed data inside a genuine situation.

The definitions in their similarity, all refer to one common interpretation. That is, AR allows the co-existence of both real and virtual objects in the same space. Virtual objects in this case, could range from simple texts, to videos, images, 3-Dimensional (3D) static and animated computer aided designs (CAD). Researchers in the past had tried to place distinctly where AR fit within the domain of reality and in 1994, this was finally clarified by Paul Milgram. According to **(Milgram and Kishino, 1994)**, AR is said to exist within the Mixed Reality domain.

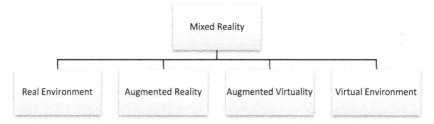

Diagrammatic description of Milgram's Reality-Virtuality Continuum. Adapted from Milgram and Kishino (1994)

Milgram searched out to make clearer the refinement between various gatherings of progressing innovative advancements. He accomplished this by part them in view of four classes of situations as found in figure 2.0 above. On the most distant left of the graph lies the genuine environment, while an absolutely immersive and profoundly captivating virtual environment lies on the far right. Milgram places AR between the Real and Virtual Environment yet nearer to the Real Environment.

This is inferable from the way that AR transfers virtual items in a way that has a tendency to superimpose the enclosing Real Environment. Enlarged Virtuality, nearer to the Virtual Environment, contrarily identifies with a case where substance from the Real Environment add to the expanded made encompassing (**Milgram and Kishino, 1994**).

2.2 AR equipment prerequisites

Setting up a fundamental AR framework would require the accompanying equipment (**Azuma, 1997; Billinghurst, Kato and Poupyrev, 2001**):

- a camcorder to catch continuous pictures,
- a solid processor, enough to composite genuine and virtual questions or venture mimicked 3D surroundings progressively,
- a critical measure of storage room to store virtual items,
- and a presentation interface to permit client association with genuine and virtual anticipated articles

These above recorded arrangement of equipment are similarly utilized by various other manmade brainpower based advancements. However, an unmistakable quality AR has over of likewise coupled advancements, is its capacity to flawlessly composite virtual items inside genuine situations, and in logically significant behavior (**Billinghurst, Kato and Poupyrev, 2001; Chang, Morreale, and Medicherla, 2010**).

2.2.1 Visualization shows gadgets

Perception presentations are an imperative bit of each AR setup. These are designed pictorial frameworks, contained visual, electronic and building coupled parts. These gadgets permit the presentation of pictures along the optical way of the onlooker. In connection to AR, it is the scaffold of visual correspondence between the eyewitness' eye and the expected expanded item (**Wang et al., 2014**). AR Display gadgets can be ordered into three, recorded and clarified underneath:

- **Handheld Displays:** These are light weight, level surfaced, Liquid Crystal Displays (LCD) that have worked in cameras to permit the representation of increased items inside a situation (**Choi and Kim, 2012**). By means of the gadget's camera, this present reality is displayed on the screen through caught video outlines, combined with the superimposed virtual items created by the AR application. With handheld gadgets, the possibility of submersion inside the expanded environment is not accomplished, as the client is bound to a consolidated perspective of the virtual and genuine environment from the gadget's screen (**Dey and Sandor, 2014**). Inundation identifies with the thought where a client feels physically display in a manufactured or expanded reality. Case of such gadgets range from Personal Digital Assistants (PDAs) to Pocket Computers and Mobile Smart Phones. The gadgets house a mix processor, interior recollections and intuitive touch screens more often than not worked by remote advances.
- **Spatial Displays:** These are gadgets that straightforwardly show visual data on any normal item (**Display gadgets, 1993**). The data is much of the time anticipated on the items with the guide of a straightforward anticipating device i.e. a Projector. It ought to be noticed that spatial showcases are additionally not immersive in nature.
- **Head Mounted Displays** (HMD): Devices of this write are worn on the head of clients to show visual data directly before their observable pathway. Engineers concocted the possibility of HMDs with an end goal to keep pictures inside a client's perspective, regardless of where their

8

heads where turned (**Hua et al., 2000**). HMDs are of two sorts: Optical and Video transparent show-cases. Optical transparent gadgets present expanded data through half straightforward reflected screens called "Combiners" while video a transparent then again, make utilization of caught video outlines. The edges are gotten using two joined scaled down cameras and serve as a foundation overlay for the expanded data (**Hua et al., 2000; Shibata, 2002**). Most HMDs are available the sentiment inundation yet all relies on upon their managed field of perspective. That is, a HMDs managed field of perspective is straightforwardly corresponding to the level of situational immersive feeling the client gets from its utilization (**Shibata, 2002**).

2.3 Field and industry implementations of ARI

AR complies with the suspicion that increasing the knowledge of a client is of a higher advantage than built computerized reasoning (Brooks, 1996). Inferable from its one of a kind representation approach, scholastics have anticipated that the innovation, in the 21st century, will get to be a stand-out amongst the most on a very basic level used applications (**Kroeker, 2010**). A forecast that is presently right now being acknowledged at an across the board rate. AR created applications as of late have not been limited, as its present usage traverse an assorted scope of attempts, some of which have been highlighted beneath.

2.3.1 Medical field

Medicinal executions of AR have been perceived subsequent to the late 1990s and a considerable measure of dynamic exploration is still done here to date (Hawkes, 1999). A portion of the effectively pragmatic archived advantages of AR usage in the field of drug incorporate (**Li, 2006**):

• The capacity to derive conclusion in view of for all intents and purposes venture life structures of patients

• Doctors can now do surgeries with AR serving as continuous aides

• The utilization of AR as instructional aides in surgeries likewise build levels of accuracy amid methods, in this way prompting many less dangers.

To bolster two or three Li's focuses, an amazing utilization of AR from a restorative application connection, identifies with the appropriation of intelligent live perceptions. Laparoscopy, otherwise called insignificantly obtrusive surgery (MIS) has turned into a more compelling system attributable to its change through the presentation of AR. This alludes to a procedural style of surgery that requires little entry points to complete operations when contrasted with conventional open surgeries. It was initially completed in 1987 and exhibited favourable circumstances of lesser draining and agony amid surgical methodology (Laparoscopic cholecystectomy., 1991). Be that as it may, the absence of direct vision remained as a noteworthy mishap to the procedure for a considerable length of time (**Botden and Jakimowicz, 2008**). In 1994, an AR venture completed at the Massachusetts

Institute of Technology **(Grimson, et al., 1996)**, prompted the formation of a navigational framework that illuminated this issue.

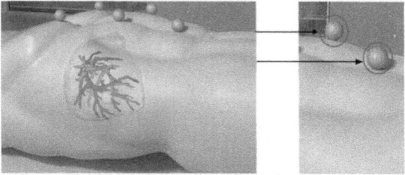

ARIS ER – 3D Virtual Surgery Guide. Source: Kalkofen, Mendez and Schmalstieg (2007)

The application called "ARIS ER" was designed to guide surgeries with the aid of virtually projected 3D scans of patient anatomies (figure 2.1). ARIS ER, which is used frequently today, asides enhancing laparoscopic procedures, has also been found to reduce the typical surgery procedure time from a lengthy 8 to 5 hours **(Grimson, et al., 1996)**. Its ability to provide an enhanced 3D view of the operated area, also enhances the precision, control and flexibility of surgical tasks **(Zhu et al., 2004; Nicolau et al., 2011)**.

2.3.2 Military field

Military planes during that time have made utilization of "Head-Up" unfurled presentations to overlay virtual scenes on genuine environment perspectives of pilots. Asides introducing guided route includes, the application helps in enrolling focuses inside the earth, in this way giving a method for exactness in pointing flying machine weapons **(Azuma, 2001)**. This current innovation has been taken the additional mile by going portable as found in figure 2.2 underneath. These days, it presents comparative capacities on the ground as it does with pilots and then some. Not just does it furnish ground troops with insights concerning checked targets, it likewise helps troops in turning away risky parts by giving a mapped outlined representation of their battle zone. This further permits separating foe soldiers from companions and helps military strategists in sorting out units the most ideal approach to make progress in missions, with insignificant losses **(Hicks, et al., 2002; Behringer, Jun and Sundareswaran, 2002)**.

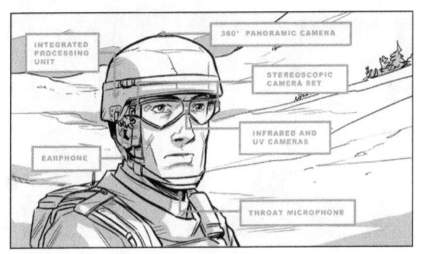

Prototype description of an AR military goggle currently being developed by Tanagram Partners. Source: Kurzweil Accelerating Intelligence (2014)

2.3.3 Retail and marketing industry

In the matter of retail, benefits are created through the offer of items, executed either from physical (block and mortar) or online areas. As a rule, item deals are helped through the start of promoting techniques did by separate retailers. Despite the fact that the acknowledgment and benefits of e-business have drastically ascended since its presentation in the mid-90s, a significant rate of retail exercises are still helped out through the customary "block and mortar" rehearse **(Datta, 2010)**. With an end goal to adjust the scales, conventional style retailers of all sizes are step by step moving towards the dynamic e-trade area. Through their relocation, these organizations all appear to confront the test of adjusting to the absence of direct communication with physical items in showcasing and deals systems **(Chaurasia, n.d.)**. Be that as it may, the expanded reception of AR as of late has been seen to facilitate this move **(Spreer and Kallweit, 2014)**. The usage of AR in the retail business is as of now giving entrepreneurs various points of interest **(Chaurasia, n.d.)**. The idea of "virtual fitting rooms" is one of such executions which has been seen to decidedly help change rates and a lessening as fair exchanges for retail attire stores **(Pachoulakis, 2012)**. Virtual fitting rooms as found in figure 2.3 underneath, present clients with a method by which they can experiment with showed items on the web.

Barbie Augmented Reality Data" We Are Organized Chaos, 29 May 2012, retrieved 4 July 2012

Garments showed are naturally superimposed on continuous video pictures of clients anticipated with the guide of their webcams. Organizations, for example, **J.C Penny and Bloomingdale** as of now utilize this innovation and have reported massive advantages in their business **(Pachoulakis, 2012).**

Asides the retail garments part, furniture organizations have likewise been taking advatage of AR to help their deals and promoting techniques. For instance, **Ingvar Kamprad, Elmtaryd and Agunnaryd (IKEA)**, a widely acclaimed furniture organization, as of late exploited AR to improve presentations of their 2014 spring item inventory. The thought was thoroughly considered to control issues of client's returning furniture that turned out the wrong size, for areas they had planned to place them. The organization, through the guide of an outsider seller built up a portable AR application to improve inventory's utilization. By this implies, clients who gain the lists are presently ready to see virtual reviews of furniture and how they fit inside their family rooms before they make their requests (see figure 2.4 underneath).

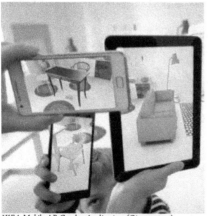

IKEA Mobile AR Catalog Application. (Gizmag, 2014)

Clients keeping in mind the end goal to use the administration, are required to download the free AR application to their shrewd gadgets, through a gave join. After introducing and the fruitful dispatch of the application, they can then centre in on orange crosses situated at the base of the inventory's picked item pages. The client is then educated through the application to put the list at the area where he or she expects to have the furniture and consequently, a 3D perspective of the chose furniture is anticipated. Measurements of each virtual furniture anticipated depend on physical sizes of those accessible in this present reality organization showroom.

2.3.4 Tourism sector

Tourism is a standout amongst the most lucrative and quickly developing commercial ventures around the world. The business depends incredibly on data and of late, innovation inputs have been required in higher requests to assume a focal part. This applies in its conveyance of data, as well as towards the improvement of general travel and sightseers' experience. Advanced sightseers progressively decide on autonomous travel, surrendering the requirement for visit guides, yet at the same time require a mode data as the trip. As an aftereffect of this, they wind up contingent upon conventional travel guides which now and again could contain out of date data, inferable from a need in the standard recurrence of their redesigns (Bellotti et al., 2005). As another option to customary print controls, the industry is presently embracing more AR advancements with an end goal to give visitors continuous data (D., E. furthermore, D., 2012). There are at present an abundance of downloadable vacationer AR applications, all in view of various geographic areas. These have generally been created by autonomous or government contracted sellers to help sightseers through their go inside different nations. Investigation is a continuous inspiration for visitors and subsequently, makes exact route a critical element. AR innovations have been known not guests with encouraged headings to destinations by anticipating virtual data on their perspectives continuously, depicting ways to take after. One of such cases is the "London Tube", a versatile AR application intended to extend visibility and closure; thereby prompting underground tube stations in London, from client current areas (see figure 2.5 underneath).

The London Tube Mobile AR Navigation App. Source: Presselite (n.d.)

Versatile AR programs are likewise a mainstream download pattern amongst visitors, so far accomplishing more than 20million downloads from enrolled application stores **(Langlotz, Grubert and Grasset, 2013)**. These programs empower travellers' entrance on-the-go data in view of physical areas through their mobiles. All data are anticipated as virtual explanations, introducing qualities and geospatial information identifying with their quick surroundings. The program distinguishes distinctive alternatives, for example, attractions, bearings, eateries and bars, interest focuses, transport joins and so forth. This gives vacationers the chance to do better educated choices as they explore **(Yovcheva et al., 2014)**. Case of such programs are **Wikitude,** which was produced in **2008** (Wikitude, 2008) and **Layar,** created in 2009 (Layar, 2009).

2.4 AR implementations from learning perspective.

In contrast with virtual reality (VR), AR is bit by bit leading the pack as a favoured instructional apparatus all in all instructive settings. This is inferable from its common convenience for teamed coordinated efforts amongst guides and understudies (Kaufmann, 2006). Through its technique for collaboration with this present reality, the innovation gives a moderately special method for handing-off guided guidelines in a for the most part worthy way **(Martín-Gutiérrez et al., 2013)**. There has been a significant inflow of distributed writing throughout the years in connection to the use of AR, from an assortment of instructive learning spaces. Be that as it may, the flow level of exploration in this course still stays to be completely investigated in tertiary training connections (Cheng and Tsai, 2012; Wu et al., 2013). For instance, **Duenser and Hornecker (2007), Dunleavy, Dede, and Mitchell (2008), Klopfer and Squire (2008), Chang, Morreale and Medicherla (2010),** all highlight prominent AR learning situations for essential and optional instructive settings. They all element material learning substance to which AR can serve as both assistive and collective apparatuses as depicted through whatever remains of this segment. The capacity to improve learning background is a zone which has yielded positive results in kids, using AR **(Chang, Morreale and Medicherla, 2010)**. Figure 2.6 underneath, portrays kids perusing a storybook mixed with intuitive enlarged it

Kids interacting with ARBook. Source: Duenser and Hornecker (2007).

The task which was started in 2007 by the British Broadcasting Corporation (BBC) was planned to assess the utilization of AR coupled books for early kid training proficiency **(Dunser and Hornecker, 2007)**. Youthful pre-school kids between the ages of 5-7, were utilized for the assessment. The youngsters, obtained from 2 group elementary schools, were assembled in sets through the study. The point was to watch their level of association, communitarian endeavours and how the framework may emphatically upgrade their perusing knowledge. Through communication with the AR Book, the kids could control the virtual characters inside the story and comprehend mystery astounds with the guide of substantial oar controls which had custom markers connected to them and the story book. Perception of increased items were accomplished with the guide of desktop PCs and outside webcams. By chatting with the youngsters, the consequences of the assessment were acquired. The result of the discussions demonstrated that AR as an option learning apparatus, was connecting with to understudies of this level, as well as demonstrated a change in their review of short occasions inside the story.

As examination in this heading went on, another one of a kind AR application was produced by **Professor's Eric Klopfer and Chris Dede (Dunleavy, Dede, and Mitchell, 2008)**. The handheld, open air, instructive gaming application, named "Outsider Contact", was intended to help both junior and senior secondary school understudies through a blend of education and scientific subjects. Arranged around an outsider intrusion situation, groups of 4 members each allocated parts, are required to team up towards setting up the intention behind the outsider appearance. The method of reasoning behind the application's configuration was to give phonetic and numerical related examples, which when recognized by understudies as they play, would attest the omnipresence and significance of dialect and arithmetic. With an end goal to think of a genuinely captivating instructive experience, the engineers subsequently exploited innate properties identifying with the subjects. This comprised of exceptional themes normally hard to handle, for example, the scientific brilliant proportion, Fibonacci arrangement and antiquated social dialects **(Klopfer and Squire, 2008)**. For instance, understudies were required to make sense of scientific riddles keeping in mind the end goal to acquire 4 digit numerical codes that give access to virtual structures where proof are covered up. The subsequent succession of codes accumulated as they associate will wind up shaping a Fibonacci grouping of numbers, which is relied upon to be acknowledged by the exploring understudies. As various arrangements of information are accumulated, the understudies get the chance to concoct differentiating reasons taking into account why the outsiders may have arrived. All proof and reasoning's assembled by every group toward the end of the activity will then be talked about with the class.

Student interacting with application on handheld computer.
Source: Klopfer and Dede (2008)

GPS receiver technology designed by Holux.
Source: Klopfer and Dede (2008)

Collaborations with the diversion was built up through the guide of a Dell Axiom versatile PC seen above in figure 2.7a. A Global Positioning System (GPS) collector as found in figure 2.7b, was likewise exploited to help in associating both understudies' genuine and virtual world areas. As the groups investigate their open air environment, a guide on the presentation gadget exhibits the virtual protests and characters that exist in the AR space, superimposed on the genuine environment. In spite of the fact that consequences of the activity displayed positive levels of learning improvement and engagement, the study was constrained as an aftereffect of relentless mistakes got from the GPS collector. Science is another subject on an evaluation school level which AR ideas have been effectively executed. It is a subject that for the most part requires pictured presentations keeping in mind the end goal to help understudies in examining originations of unique nature (**Birk, 1996**). These originations could identify with the auxiliary types of particles and atoms, which normally can't be seen with the human eyes (**Justi and Gilbert, 2002**). **Chang, Morreale and Medicherla (2010)** depicted a virtual AR lab for Chemistry which scientists from the Switzerland Federation Institute of Technology (SFIT) in had thought of. The framework titled "Enlarged Chemistry" presents clients with the chance to see and gather straightforward auxiliary particles and atoms politeness of custom AR markers, outside webcams and desktop PCs. The noticeable iotas can then have connected to frame particles by intertwining the external electrons of picked molecules with those that match its suitable shell. To build up the production of particles, markers relegated to individual iotas must be acquired close nearness to each different as found in figure 2.8 underneath.

New molecular structures formed from the fusion of virtual atoms assigned to individual markers.
Source: Cheng Morreale and Medicherla (2010)

Upon a successful fusion, a new molecular structure is formed and more atoms can be combined utilizing the same explained process. Inclusively, labels providing the names of molecular structures formed, pop-up upon their successful creation. Through this means, students are allowed the affordance to come up with complex molecular structures of their own, but are still restricted to the sub-atomic laws of molecular interactivity. As compared to the traditionally inclined methods of building molecular models from "Straws" and "Styrofoam", an enhanced advantage towards learning was presented through the use of this technology. Positive results from its implementation in line with increased student motivation were also documented from evaluating of the application with students at Saint George's Secondary School in Switzerland.

2.4.1 The need for more research in the educational field

Irrespective of the numerous documented success implementation stories narrated above, Cheng and Tsai (2012) and Wu et al. (2013) assert that continuous research in the field of education is still a necessity. This is towards establishing a fully adequate differentiation between the technology and its counterparts in all levels of education. At the moment, the benefits of AR in terms of learning enhancements, are yet to be fully realized within tertiary levels of education. In comparison to studies undertaken on much more established technologies in tertiary education settings such as VR, research of AR applications and proof of its effects as an instructional tool still appears quite superficial (The Application of Augmented Reality in Education Compared to Virtual Reality, 2013). According to observations from Blake & Butcher-Green (2009), El Sayed et al. (2011) and Wu et al. (2013), most of the AR research carried out to date from tertiary educational contexts have been targeted mostly at design based approaches, usability and emerging implementation trends. Another standout theme detected amongst empirical studies on this level relates to the fact that research related designs have relatively been simple, carried out with small samples and were short-term in their exploratory nature. Various studies come across through the review of existing literatures were also at their early stages of development and were dependent on students' self-reports of usability and efficiency towards establishing AR associated learning effects. Construct3D (Kaufmann, Schmalstieg and Wagner, 2000; Kauffmann, 2002; Kaufmann and Schmalstieg, 2003; Kaufmann et al., 2005; Kaufmann, 2009), CONNECT (Arvanitis et al., 2007; Arvanitis et al., 2011) and Gen-1 (Behzadan and Kamat, 2012) are notable examples of discovered AR tools, for which empirical studies were carried out from a tertiary education perspective. The three cases presented below cite different shortcomings in the level of evaluation carried out to towards establishing their effectiveness in tertiary education learning.

Construct3D is an AR tutoring tool developed in Austria by Professor's Hanes Kaufmann and Dietmar Schmalstieg. The application was conceived specifically to help educate university students in mathematical geometry by taking advantage of 3D geometric designed models (Kaufmann,

Schmalstieg and Wagner, 2000). It provides users with the ability to collaborate and design simple primitives such as cones, lines, spheres, points, cubes and cylinders, within the same virtual space, viewed through the aid of a HMD as seen in figure 2.9 below.

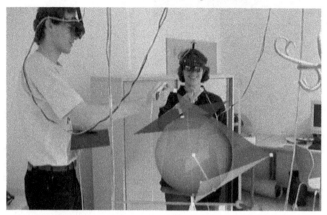

A visiting tutor and Student interacting with the application within the development lab.
Source: Kaufmann, Schmalstieg and Wagner (2000)

Construction actions within the application were accomplished with direct manipulation in 3D space through the use of handheld computers and tracked styli provided with 6 degrees of freedom. Designed primitive modifications within the virtual space were also made available, inclusive of other essential operations such as primitive type selections and deletions. Construct 3D was an application basically designed for guided exploration between 2 participants, one being the tutor and the other a student. In 2000, owing to the fact that the application was still in its early stages of development, the researchers pointed out that an evaluation in a proper class setting could not be established (Kaufmann, Schmalstieg and Wagner, 2000). They also did note that visiting tutors and students alike were given the opportunity try out the system and this provided them with regular and valuable feedback through its development. Further exploration in literature (Kauffmann, 2002; Kaufmann and Schmalstieg, 2003; Kaufmann et al., 2005; Kaufmann, 2009) relating to the application however, showed no evidence of an extended research and hence its significance within a tertiary learning environment could not be verified.

The CONNECT AR educational instruction tool, developed in 2007, was a European Union funded project. The application was designed with the aim of unifying both institutions and Science centers, through a combination of novel-based AR and web-based streaming technologies, towards the support of learning in various settings (Arvanitis et al., 2007). The interactive environment encourages students to stop over at science centers and carry out experiments virtually not possible in schools. The students can also further develop on their experiences gained either back at school or their homes through the aid of augmentations relayed by web related streaming methods. The researchers took advantage of a Mobile wearable computer and HMD visualization system in establishing the mediated AR application as seen in figure 2.10 below.

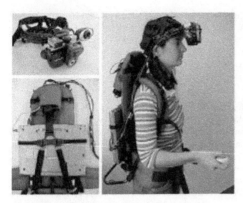

CONNECT AR device setup. Source: Arvanitis et al. (2007)

By this means, the CONNECT AR application delivers mixed reality solutions based on various science related teachings (Arvanitis et al., 2007). Relating to Physics for example, it augments virtual contents such as the process of land and sea breeze and magnetic force variables which are normally invisible to the naked eyes in real world view (Arvanitis et al., 2007). In order to evaluate the system, the researchers decided to focus on usability (wearability level) and teaching effectiveness, using a combination of both abled and physically challenged participants. Though results from comparison of both sets of participants presented similar positive outcomes, the sample size of participants used was quite limited (a combination of 5 physically challenged and 5 able students). Researchers however went on to stress that irrespective of the sample size used, the results were still of significance, keeping in mind the obvious room for further work. Further investigations in this case revealed a documented upgrade of the system in terms of additional subjects catered for (Arvanitis et al., 2011), but there were no cases of an improved evaluation carried out.

Gen-1 as described by its developers Professor's Ahmed Behzadan and Vineet Kamat, is an enhanced prototyped AR Book. It is was developed to aid Civil Engineering students at the University of Central Florida gain a much better insight in terms of the various types of construction machinery available in the field (Behzadan and Kamat, 2012). In order to achieve this, custom designed AR markers were employed to help overlay 3D models of existing machineries in real space. Figure 2.11 below depicts an example of a lesson from the prototype Gen-1 AR book.

Gen-1 AR Book sample page. Source: Behzadan and Kamat (2012)

As seen in the figure above, each page on the left hand of the book is associated with an equivalent right hand page that consists of an AR marker. Students can read through the text and view the regular 2D images situated within the book in the traditional manner, but when placed under an

AR visualization display, the corresponding 3D model of the particular machinery is presented. Outputs of the Gen-1 AR book which come in both static and animated forms, can be viewed either with the aid of a webcam connected to a computer screen or through a HMD. In terms of evaluation relating to Gen-1's effectiveness on students in learning environments, there has been none carried out to date on the system. However, according to the literature, only proof of concept experiments have been attempted and the researchers are looking towards full scale implemented usability evaluations (Behzadan and Kamat, 2012).

From the above detailed examples, an obvious lack in research completeness can be observed. It highlights the fact that more justifiable evidence in relation to the educational values of AR within tertiary level contexts are required. This can only be achieved through more controlled and in-depth empirical studies carried out with larger samples and credible instrumentations. Hence, the present study attempts to add to the continuously increasing collection of research in this field, by verifying that the use of AR can create a much more enhanced learning environment for tertiary level students. In order to achieve this comparison, a cost effective mobile AR application has been developed for learning purposes using the same content within a selected conventional teaching material. Additionally, an important assumption over the years in relation to learners, involves the source and level of motivation to learn. Motivation stands as a crucial factor within educational settings. It is believed that high levels of motivation are most often essential for success (Kuznetsov and Kuznetsova, 2011; McCartney, 2013; Martin, Galentino and Townsend, 2014). It has also been established that the integration of interactive technologies such as assistive mobile and stationary computing devices within learning settings, make the process of learning more enjoyable and approachable for students (Brush and Saye, 2004; Hillman, 2013; Chuang, 2014). Therefore, from an AR perspective, the study will also be seeking to establish if its implementation can positively influence motivation and possibly lead to its acceptance within the learning environment.

2.4.2 Hypothesis and research implications

It is hypothesized that the use of AR as an instructional treatment, will enhance student learning and present a significant difference in learning gains, compared to traditional learning methods. Additionally, an analytic assessment of students' motivation and acceptance is also important towards determining the strengths and weaknesses of AR as a technological learning tool. Results of the study, if positive, will be used to improve the teaching curriculum at the National level in Mauritius. This will however require further ethical approval for an extended research.

CHAPTER 3: DESIGN PROCEDURE AND CONSIDERATIONS

The accompanying section gives in subtle elements, a review of the AR Brain application's configuration reason and idea. It likewise reveals insight into contemplations regarding demonstrating and improvement stage decisions that postured huge towards imagining and evaluating the application.

3.1 The concept

The mind is regularly referred to by neuroscientists as the most amazingly complex organ of the human framework **(Cassan, 2006; Vera-Portocarrero, 2007)**. That being said, the thought to make an AR application taking into account its life systems, was gotten from the way that such an organ requires an exact spatial representation of its structure. The standard way to deal with study in most instructive settings depend enormously on 2D representational materials. This can have credited to the way that it remains as the most straightforward open coaching help. Hence, the fruitful handing-off of anatomical subtle elements through this technique is intensely subject to the capacity of understudies to change inside their brains, the 2D data they get to 3D keen understandings. As indicated by **(Luursema et al., 2006)**, this required subjective change is typically a significant undertaking for understudies to ace.

The **ARBrain** is a portable enlarged reality application created with the point of helping clients in finding out about the human mind and its related parts. (Gilbert, Blessing and Blankenship, 2009) expressed that learning results are improved in situations where understudies are given the freedom to openly control and investigate ideas voluntarily. This gives space for a more inside and out perception of spatial data, and consequently, a superior comprehension of the related thought being displayed. The application with an end goal to fulfil this essential gives client a method by which they can completely interface with a 3D spatial perspective of the human cerebrum. This association is bolstered through the empowered affordance of element controls, for example, turning and scaling highlights. The application additionally gives clients the decision of dismembering the mind with a specific end goal to further view its interior parts. This dismemberment gives them sidelong and average perspectives of the model. Names and portrayals are accessible for the understudies, found both on the horizontal and average locales of the model as they investigate. These districts of printed data mapped to the diverse parts of the 3D model, can be uncovered and disguised alternatively whenever by clients of the application. The thought behind this was to promote give a feeling of control, all in view of client investigation inclinations.

3.2 Application requirements

So as to commence the venture, the necessities required to be met by the application were built up and explored with the undertaking director. These incorporated the accompanying:
- The planned 3D model should have been as reasonable and definite as could be allowed, showing the most essential outside and inside parts of the human mind.
- The application ought to give clients clear and digitally succinct data.
- Room for investigation and the capacity to unreservedly control the expanded model was to be made accessible.
- The application needed to give a proficient level of responsiveness to client activities and charges.
- Marker(s) on which the 3D Brain model is anticipated, ought to not the slightest bit hinders a client's perspective. That is, the model ought to be completely superimposed on the highest point of the marker.
- Finally, the application's interface must be alluring and engaging. Clients should likewise have the capacity to associate with the interface at first look with practically zero many-sided quality in its use.

3.3 Software design considerations

3.3.1 3D modelling platform

Keeping in mind the end goal to finish the displaying part of the undertaking, a blend of Maya and Z-Brush were chosen as the stages of decision. The Autodesk Maya programming is an amazingly skilled system which helps makes bewildering exact 3D models and intelligent liveliness. In spite of the fact that Maya can be coordinated as far as capacities with a couple of other 3D outline programming in the business sector, the decision was made particularly inferable from existing information and commonality with stage. It ought to be noticed that Maya was planned from the onset as an expert demonstrating instrument, which makes it badly designed for first time clients to control. It requires a sound measure of devotion to handle its full capacities and accordingly, may not be the best decision for apprentices. Z-Brush on the other, which is additionally a 3D demonstrating programming was chosen essentially for its oversimplified, simple to utilize but high-determination chiselling results. However, with regards to top to bottom specifying, the product misses the mark, prompting the purpose behind their blend. The thought was to outline an exceptionally reasonable model and with just Maya, the way toward accomplishing that would have been significantly additional tedious. Actually, models etched in Z-Brush can be foreign made over to Maya for constant improvement and the other way around. Hence, Z-Brush was acquainted with shape the general state of the model, while got done with specifying was to be taken care of in Maya. Both programming requires licenses which were obtained keeping in mind the end goal to exploit their full abilities.

3.3.2 Application development platform

Inferable from the same inclination for commonality, the Processing open source advancement environment emerged as first decision to complete the application's improvement. Not at all like Maya, Processing upon its configuration, was basically proposed for less educated software engineers to comprehend the essentials of PC programming ideas. It has following risen above from its unique reason and has been used by pretty much any personalities or people with programming aptitudes to make intuitively determined model programming. The greatest advantage about using this environment is the way that it is moderately simple to control and gives space for designers of any class to concoct intuitive and graphically determined applications. With respect to enlarging reality through the Processing stage, four fundamental libraries were required:

- **OPENGL:** The OPENGL library is an inner coordinated library in the handling advancement bundle. It is fundamentally in charge of empowering handling's 3D programming capacities as it gives the earth to which virtual planned substance can be melded into 3D encompass space.

- **JMyron:** The JMyron library is additionally an outsider library for the handling environment which gives space for obvious article control without the need of hard coding. Actualized with the handling environment, it serves as a video catch and vision augmentation. More or less, it adds to the framework by presenting elements, for example, movement and shading related following of items inside the 3D space.

- **OBJLoader:** The OBJLoader outsider library is an obj 3D document expansion loader required in handling. This configuration is the main way handling and a couple of other advancement stages can acknowledge and stack imported 3D models. Actually, OBJ organizations are content related documents which hold coordinate depictions of 3D model vertices. These directions' help preparing see how to draw or present the demonstrated article in the 3D environment. After sending out a 3D model in OBJ group, the record is likewise for the most part created with a mtl document expansion which holds surface related mapping points of interest of the sent out model.

- **NyARToolkit** for Processing: The **NyARToolkit** for Processing is an outsider library reached out from one of the **ARToolworks'** group of programming (ARToolkit for Java). The library was created particularly to work in the Processing environment towards enlarging reality. With the guide of the **NyARToolkit**, 3D models are superimposed unto this present reality by means of live video and its marker-based identification highlights. It fills in as takes after:
  o A webcam catches genuine live video which is transferred to the associated PC.
  o The **NyARToolkit** library has influence by empowering the AR application to seek through the caught video outlines for any conspicuous markers.
  o For any markers distinguished, the library permits the application to perform algorithmic scientific capacities. This is important with a specific end goal to figure out where the webcam is situated, in respect to the distinguished dark squared areas of the marker.
  o Upon deciding the webcam's position, the 3D model to be anticipated is then drawn from the precise position of the webcam.
  o The anticipated 3D model is drawn on the caught video of this present reality environment, making it seem stuck to the assigned marker.
  o This coming about yield is introduced to the viewer with the guide of a presentation innovation.

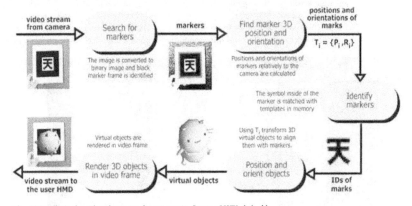

The ARToolkit's algorithm driven tracking scenario. Source: HITLab (n.d.)

Figure 3.1 above provides a graphical display of the **NyARToolkit's** marker detection and model projection display.

3.3.3 Issues detected with Processing

Regardless of Processing's prior highlighted abilities (area (3.3.2)), misfortunes were experienced through the task's underlying advancement stages, because of the accompanying reasons:

- The **NyARtoolkit** library was found to be inconsistent with (2.x.x) renditions of Processing, because of an adjustment in Processing's API. In different examples where the library was foreign made to Processing and run, it generally prompted a **NullPointerException** when calling the "**showObject()**" technique for the **NyARToolkit** inside class as found in figure 3.2 beneath. **NullPointerExceptions** experienced in Processing, for the most part mean a particular blunder has happened in the system. For this situation, "calling the occurrence strategy "**showObject()**" of an assumed invalid article", prompted the blunder.

- **NullPointerException** event as a consequence of **NyARToolkit's** inconsistency with 2.x.x adaptations of Processing

- he first issue was worked around by minimizing on the renditions list till a more perfect variant was found (v1.5.1). For this situation, the application appeared to begin, yet dependably slammed following a few moments referring to an **OutOfMemoryError** found in figure 3.3 underneath. This special case happens in examples where there is inadequate memory accessible to run a system.

- **OutOfMemoryError** event because of inadequate distributed memory to the system

- The memory limit issue was illuminated by expanding the most extreme arbitrary access memory (RAM) assigned to Processing, with a specific end goal to suit the application's need. In any case, it worked out that the (1.5.1) adaptation of Processing, did not permit utilization of more than 1024MB. In spite of the fact that the application could now be run, the memory dispensed still demonstrated lacking for the models, and highlighted the last issue.

- When a marker is perceived and the comparing 3D model relegated to it is rendered, the polygon networks (gathering of vertices) that make up the model were apparently noticeable. This introduced them in a harsh structure than anticipated and happened as a consequence of the way that they demonstrated excessively nitty gritty for Processing's rendering capacities. A case of the subsequent rendered item is found in figure 3.4 underneath.

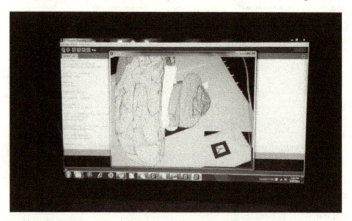

Roughly rendered initial projection of 3D brain model owing Processing's inability to its depth in detail

The specialist exhibited these deficiencies to the venture administrator and it was concurred certain that an option stage for advancement was required.

3.3.4 The alternative

A couple of other improvement stages were found in the early phases of the task and must be re-examined taking after the inadequacies recognized in Processing. The decision of programming now needed to meet necessities drawn from both the advantaged and burdened characteristics of Processing. The table beneath presentations a correlation of accessible programming comprehensive of Processing, from which the last decision was made.

Requirements	Adobe Flash	C++ OpenFrame-work	Unity	Processing
3rd Party AR Development Extension	FLARToolkit	ARToolkit	Vuforia, UAR-Toolkit	nyARToolkit
3D Modelling Capability	No	No	Yes	No
Deployment Option(s)	No	No	Yes (Android, IOS, Windows, Standalone, Web)	Yes (Android)
Sufficient memory affordance for application development	Yes	Yes	Yes	No
Ability to render heavily detailed models	No	Yes	Yes	No
Learning Curve	High	High	Medium	Medium

Measuring the choices showed in table 3.1, Unity emerged as the best option for the venture's continuation. Solidarity is a 3D plan stage comprising of an in-fabricated incorporated advancement environment (IDE) and a diversion motor to permit the execution of developed applications. It was chosen as the centre of the task's usage attributable to the way that it exceptionally very much gave answers for the inconveniences experienced with Processing. Solidarity additionally displayed the ability to code in C#, which like java, permitted the application to be effortlessly extendable. This extensibility is owed to its article situated (OO) nature. In spite of the fact that it is conceivable to make alterations to all applications, just those which can keep up their unique structure and take in extra changes are practically esteemed extendable (Members, 2014). Contrasted with procedural style programming, the OO approach made actualizing changes through the advancement arranges a great deal less demanding with negligible interruption on the application. The decision of an extendable outline was likewise an advantage to the task's iterative advancement style as it gave space for the execution of required functionalities in little strides through the undertaking's lifecycle. Its 3D demonstrating capacities likewise demonstrated an essential preferred standpoint through improvement. At specific focuses, changes were required on the officially composed model and these were effortlessly proficient on Unity's stage instead of importing the model back to Maya. Solidarity was an apparatus that had not been wandered in the past but rather accomplishment in its usage must be ascribed to the abundance of instructional exercises and dynamic gatherings devoted to the application.

3.3.5 Unity and AR advancement with Vuforia

Solidarity offered outsider libraries in any semblance of Vuforia and **UARToolkit** as choices for taking care of AR parts of the application's configuration. In spite of the fact that a variant of the **ARToolkit** had at first been used with Processing and consistently would have been less demanding to proceed with, **Vuforia** displayed a specific quality that prompted its thought. Working with renditions of the **ARToolkit,** it was watched that edge rates appeared to drop fundamentally as representation situations were caught. This added to a block in smooth cooperation's while following doled out markers for 3D model showcase. The favourable position Vuforia gave was a more note-worthy proficiency in accomplishing higher casing rates contrasted with the **UARToolkit**, further prompting a superior client experience.

3.3.5.1 Vuforia's following calculation clarified

Vuforia works by following corners of extraordinarily planned markers alluded to as casing markers. There are 512 pre-set up casing markers enlisted to **Vuforia**, with each marker having a particular double coded design over its fringes as found in figure 3.5 beneath.

Vuforia's standard frame markers

Interpreting a marker by **Vuforia** moderately pauses for a moment measure of preparing force, along these lines making the likelihood for each of the 512 accessible examples to be keep running in a solitary application. Multi-following is likewise made conceivable attributable to its handling productivity, and in fact a most extreme of 5 edge markers can be found and at the same time followed **(Qualcomm, 2014)**.

Vuforia's following calculation fills in as depicted beneath **(Drummond, 2011):**

- The picked marker(s) to be followed have been pre-dissected utilizing an adjusted variant of the Features from Accelerated Segment Test (FAST) consolidated in **Vuforia (Ed-wardrosten.com, 2014).** Quick is a composed calculation, produced with the end goal of finding interest focuses on articles. The unmistakable paired coded designs over the casing marker's fringes serve as the interest focuses to be distinguished, and are put away in a database. This information is then utilized for following and recognition occasions (Reference information).
- With an accumulation of reference information as of now put away in the framework, video sustains from a gadget can then be inspected progressively to match references. **Vuforia's** corner finder instrument inspects any casing marker(s) present in the video bolster and analyses distinguished focuses against its own pre-figured reference information in quest for matches.
- Upon finding an adequate number of coordinated focuses, a change network which maps the focuses in the reference marker's picture to that distinguished in the video food is approximated. This is accomplished utilizing blunder decrease techniques.
- Finally, the camera posture is resolved from the change network along these lines giving the fitting point of view and plot for the 3D model to be anticipated in the video encourage.

3.3.5.2 Deciding edge markers over custom picture targets

Vuforia likewise gives the capacity to track any custom picture focus set up of edge markers. Upon examination it was found that the way toward following custom pictures was very like that of edge markers with the exception of one disadvantage. On account of custom pictures, the framework has no reference information to work with and endeavours to discover instilled designs on the picture keeping in mind the end goal to make sense of the right yield for rehashed examples. As a consequence of this, custom pictures are required to be of a high determination furthermore should have numerous unmistakable elements to serve as interest focuses for powerful following. On the off chance that a custom picture needs such qualities, following and recognizing it would be an exhausting and at times, incomprehensible errand. Outline markers then again, don't require these qualities for successful following. As highlighted in the past segment (3.3.5.1), their twofold encoded corners are the main obliged ranges to be distinguished when followed. The region inside the dark fringe of any casing marker is for all intents and purposes of no importance to the following procedure and consequently, can be altered by designer's inclination as found in figure 3.6 beneath. Regarding downsides, the main referred to limitation they introduce identify with the way that exclusive the 512 enlisted markers can be used in an application. This however can be contended to be entirely enough as most created applications scarcely require outline markers in expansive adds up to work. Ideally, they are customized to be rapid, where one marker plays out various activities keeping in mind the end goal to restrain the sum required for the application's diverse capacities.

Example of a custom designed marker

3.4 Choice of hardware and justification

With the objective to improve learning and boost understudy engagement, cautious thought must be taken in regards to the decision of showcase, while likewise remembering cost suggestions. The cost ramifications of AR have generally remained as a boundary towards its reception inside the instruction area **(Champion, 2006; Lee, 2012)**. This has additionally been in charge of the restricting the measure of exploration completed throughout the years. In any case, with the now multiplied expansion in AR proficient cell phones and tablets have given the idea the ideal vehicle to lead the focal point of the audience, as a commanding apparatus in instruction.

For the fruitful usage of this study, it was essential for all members to do the analysis in the meantime. This would require a good setup environment comprising of quantities of the picked show gadget, enough to provide food for the normal specimen populace. Contemplating this, the idea of portable sending emerged as the most practical choice. This depended on the way that it demonstrated more financially savvy to execute, contrasted with gaining main role innovations, for example, HMDs and advanced PCs. Cell phones are intended to be light weighted, exhibiting characteristics of both versatility and opportunity of control. Their preparing and realistic rendering qualities nowadays, likewise tend to coordinate those of enhanced PCs, making them similarly perfect to work with any AR application. The idea of versatile expanded reality additionally supports a "bring your own gadget" (BYOD) rehearse. It exhibits a situation where understudies get the chance to join their own gadgets, for use inside the learning environment, in this manner quelling any issues identifying with equipment innovation adjustment.

Solidarity's capacity to send created applications on portable stages would not have been quite a bit of favourable position if **Vuforia** was not built in accordance with this reason. In conjunction with Unity, the augmentation gives backing to both IOS and Android local improvement inclinations, displaying effectively compact applications to both working stages. These stages additionally rule the portable advancements market, making them a fitting establishment for improvement. With respects gadget inclination, tablets were sensibly chosen to be the perfect decision for presentation as they tend to come in standard visible resolutions. This exhibited a minor misfortune to the BYOD rule as not all understudies were relied upon to have tablet like gadgets. It was set up through testing a scope of versatile stages that clients who had littler determination gadgets won't not infer the same level of involvement in accordance with representation of literary information. Be that as it may, through the iterative advancement arranges, a workable arrangement was inferred and this is talked about further in area (4.2) of the following part.

CHAPTER 4: DEVELOPING THE ARBRAIN APPLICATION

This part points of interest the improvement steps conveyed towards accomplishing the completely useful AR Brain application. It further goes ahead to highlight contemplations that were thoroughly considered towards its fruitful execution.

4.1 Constructing the 3D brain model

Keeping in mind the end goal to accomplish the required model, graphically point by point 3D pictures of the human cerebrum were searched out to serve as reference aides through the development procedure.

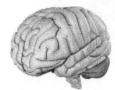 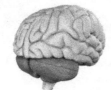 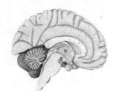

Frontal lateral view of 3D brain image   *Hind lateral view of 3D brain image*   *Medial view of 3D brain image*

a   B   c

These pictures found in figure 4.1 above were then dissected and first had an outside outlined utilizing the Z-Brush demonstrating programming. An unpleasant state of the outside segment of the cerebrum was cut out and etched by of the reference pictures utilizing Z-Brush's chiselling brush device. This included expelling and moving vertices all together accomplish a close copy. Vertices allude to corners of the underlying 3D shape spoke to in figure 4.2a beneath. Figure 4.2b then again, delineates the ultimate result after further expulsion and control of vertices.

 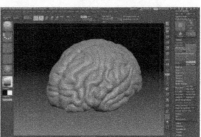

Initial mold of 3D brain model with obtained with a few vertices to outline the structure   *Final outcome upon further manipulation requiring the inclusion of more vertices*

a   b

The model now, was sent out and tried on an underlying script sent in Processing. As prior expressed in area (3.3.3), it was seen to be a bit excessively definite (thick) to process' rendering capacity. This happened as a consequence of the way that the underlying configuration was comprised of excessively numerous polygon sub-divisions (1,345,352) found in figure 4.3 underneath, and accordingly must be lessened.

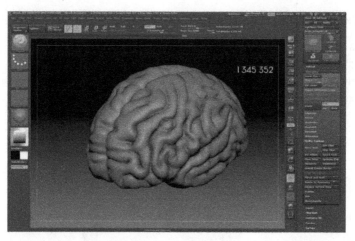

1st stage of design consisting of 1,345,352 polygon sub-divisions

Bringing down the polygon check of the model required a procedure called Retopology. This is a normal part of customary displaying work processes. By and large, models are typically developed laying hugeness on exact structure and inside and out subtle elements. This however requires extremely thick polygon networks, which could demonstrate wasteful relying upon the main role of the model. Be that as it may, through retopology, an indistinguishable lessened determination network coordinating the precise type of the at first made cross section can be accomplished.

Endless supply of the principal retopology process, the model was again tried in Processing yet at the same time demonstrated very thick for the application even lessened to 21,036 polygon subdivisions (found in figure 4.4 beneath). This unavoidably added to the choice to search out an option improvement stage (segment (3.3.4)). Retopology has a point of confinement to how far it can be completed before the model starts to lose its profundity in quality. This was impossible as protecting the model's practical subtle elements was of equivalent need towards accomplishing an effective client involvement with the application.

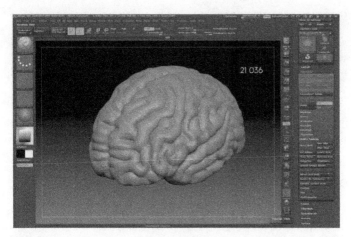

Polygon subdivision count reduced to 21,036 after retopology process. (There is a visible reduction in model density as compared to the initial presented in figure4.3 above)

Proceeding onward, the last etched outside part of the model was then traded to Maya for persistent specifying. This required cutting the outside into zones comprising of the Left and Right Hemispheres, having the four projections stretching out to every half. The Motor Cortex, Broca's and Wrenicke's ranges separately, were then cut into the left side of the equator and surfaces were connected to every zone. Finishing identifies with painting the model's surface and for this situation, was done keeping in mind the end goal to introduce a more particular mapping for every area of the cerebrum as showed in figure 4.5.

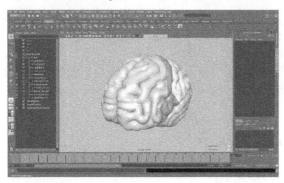

2ⁿᵈ stage of 3D model design after texturing procedure

Upon the fulfilment of the outside, the critical inside areas were followed up on. The Cerebellum, Corpus Callosum, Hippocampus, Amygdala and Pituitary Gland were etched and finished to fit the general configuration. Barring the Hippocampus and Amygdala, just half calculated segments of alternate parts were etched. They were then copied and converged on every sides of the average perspectives to re-enact an immaculate partition when analysed. Figure 4.6 beneath show occurrences of both full and dismembered cerebrum models. As found in figure 4.6b, the Hippocampus and Amygdala are the main segments that are not displayed as dismembered in the average rendition of the model.

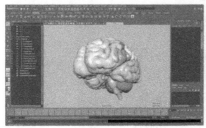

Angled lateral view of 3D model

3rd stage of design. (Angled medial view of 3D model depicting additional sculpted regions)

a   b

4.1.1 Incorporating textual data

Directly after the chiselling of every single anatomical component, marks (titles) and expressive content must be doled out to every individual segment of the model. Firstly, the model and portrayals accumulated, had their level of rightness checked by a speaker in brain science at the University. The separate segment titles, combined with the sourced portrayals were then overlaid on box networks and appended to their objective areas. Cross sections are a gathering of vertices that characterize a part of a 3D model and for this situation, were laid out in layered arrangements to permit the inclination of debilitating/empowering their perceivability on the application. The marked composed box cross sections were likewise finished to coordinate the particular districts on the model they spoke to, for a steady look. Moreover, the characterized titles and portrayals must be copied on both sides of the crates as occurrences of pivot were considered. This was executed to permit meaningfulness of every literary dat from any point the model was to be seen from the application. Figure 4.7 underneath demonstrates an analysed occasion of the finished model with every printed data effectively executed.

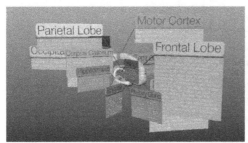

4th stage of design depicting successful textual data incorporation

The model was tried upon the consideration of every literary data, on an underlying script of the centre application which was presently being created on the Unity stage. This was vital keeping in mind the end goal to get a vibe of what's in store when envisioned from a cell phone. On two chose tablet gadgets (the Samsung Galaxy tab 3 and the Asus T100), the model was consummately anticipated and every single literary data could be imagined in insignificant helped room conditions. The light dark surface utilized on the portrayal network boxes (see figure 4.9) did not appear to compliment the white decided for the depiction content. In a controlled light environment, every single literary data was seen plainly, yet when pictured in a brighter room, light discharges appeared to display the light shade of dark utilized on the foundation as verging on white. This made intelligibility of the depiction message verging on incomprehensible.

For littler gadgets in the scope of cell phones, the Samsung Galaxy S3 and the HTC One M8 were utilized to test perceivability of the enlarged model. For this situation, the model was likewise unmistakably anticipated on both gadgets, attributable to the prior disclosed choice to save its profundity of point of interest. Literary information then again was not all around transferred. The writings were exhibited somewhat obscured independent of light conditions and required some visual strain for a decent read. In spite of the fact that scaling functionalities were to be actualized on the application, its main role was for better survey of marginally shrouded structures of the model and not as a matter of course printed information. This must be seen actually with no scaling required and subsequently, a contrasting option to its underlying usage must be made sense of.

As prior portrayed, every single printed dat on the application were at first made as cross sections which were found not to be show well-disposed on gadgets of littler resolutions. Relating the issue with kindred fashioners on the Unity designers' discussion, a thought of changing over the cross sections to high determination pictures was given as a workable arrangement. This required the cross section boxes and messages to be outlined outside of Maya in a picture altering programming, then re-imported into the project. Evidently various fashioners on the discussion had experienced comparative issues with displayed writings and the option was a win. To complete this, the Adobe Photoshop CS6 picture altering programming was chosen for the change. The cases and messages for every area were then separately upgraded, with the foundation depiction boxes changed over to a much darker shade of dim. They were then blended and spared in high determination versatile system representation (PNG) configurations to be foreign made once more into Maya. The last item was incorporated once again into the model to enhance the perspective as seen underneath in figure 4.8.

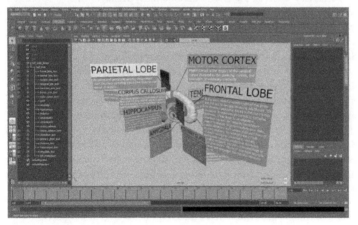

Model presentation after rework

4.2 Developing the application centre

4.2.1 Development environment setup process

Before initiating the application's development, the improvement environment must be appropriately setup. Solidarity is not an open source improvement stage but rather contains both a free and ace adaptation. The free form accompanies essential components initiated and takes into account IOS and Android versatile sending, making it all around ok to handle most yet not the majority of the undertaking's needs. The professional rendition then again displayed propelled highlights that were required and couldn't be overlooked. It was in this manner important to secure a permit for the item.

After an effective establishment of Unity, the **Vuforia** outsider augmentation was then downloaded **(https://developer.vuforia.com/assets/sdk/solidarity)** and separated into the application. The procedure of extraction was finished by unfastening the document into Unity's undertaking root index. The augmentation accompanied bundle resources comprising of various specimen extends that could be at first hurry to see direct case of its abilities. These benefits were moved to the Standard Assets envelope, an area where all bundles are put away on Unity. Toward the end of this procedure, 7 solidarity bundles recorded beneath were consequently produced.

- **vuforia-solidarity android-ios.unitypackage:** this contains the base Qualcomm Augmented Reality (QCAR) augmentation and outer datasets for target administration.
- **vuforia-solidarity android-ios-imagetargets.unitypackage:** this comprises of an example venture accomplished with the utilization of an Image Target, anticipating a basic demonstrated item
- **vuforia-solidarity android-ios-framemarkers.unitypackage:** in this specimen venture, has the same idea as the picture target bundle yet for this situation, a casing marker is used (contrasts between edge markers and picture targets have been talked about before in segment (3.3.5.2)).
- **vuforia-solidarity android-ios-multitargets.unitypackage:** this specimen venture exhibits the utilization of Multi Targets inside a situation.
- **vuforia-solidarity android-ios-virtualbuttons.unitypackage:** another specimen venture exhibiting the utilization of Virtual Buttons. In this situation, rectangular districts are made on a picture target. These areas trigger occasions when physically touched in perspective of the camera.
- **vuforia-solidarity android-ios-backgroundtextureaccess.unitypackage:** an example venture where surfaces as video foundation impacts are executed.
- **vuforia-solidarity android-ios-occlusionmanagement.unitypackage:** an example venture showing impacts of impediment utilizing straightforward shaders. These shaders through an impediment impact, permit clients an incomplete look inside genuine articles through virtual overlaid models.

To ensure the **Vuforia** expansion was legitimately stacked, each of the example ventures produced were gathered in Unity's surroundings. As proposed, aggregation of all ventures demonstrated effective, showing no fabricate blunders, and thus the earth was viewed as set for AR improvement. This now comprised of the amusement motor gave by Unity to encourage the rendering of every one of the 3D articles and application rationale, combined with AR segments in the QCAR bundle gave by **Vuforia.** The expansion of this bundle additionally naturally produced another menu in Unity, which gave access to important documentation, alongside helpful target dataset names and their properties.

4.2.2 The venture creation

At this stage, another task was made from Unity's record menu titled "Unity3D-ARBrain". The hyphen utilized as a part of between the title was incorporated to stay away from issues finding the undertaking when building. Solidarity reads white spaces and in this manner requires exceptional characters, for example, hyphens and underscores to fill any current crevices. The production of the task further prompted the opening of another venture window as seen beneath in figure 4.9. Exceptionally vital areas have been highlighted and are clarified further beneath.

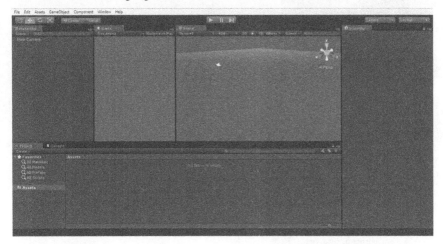

Unity 3D project development space

- **The Scene Editor** - this board is essentially where everything fabricated can be seen. It shows what is displayed to clients at runtime. Various scenes can be made, much the same as amusements have products levels.
- **The Scene Hierarchy** - this board shows each article (i.e. 3D objects) in a specific scene combined with their connections to each other.
- **The Game Renderer** - this board introduces a sneak peak of how the application looks and functions along phases of improvement, without deploying it.
- **Project Assets** - this board as the name infers, is the place all undertaking resources imported can be discovered, comprehensive of **Vuforia's**. Models, surfaces and every single composed script for application will likewise be found here.
- **Inspector Panel** - this last board shows all settings ascribed to scenes or resources chose. It can best be portrayed as the board where changes in accordance with scenes and resources are done.

The workspace was then modified to suit the analyst's inclination and the at first **extracted vuforia-solidarity android-ios.unitypackage**, was migrated to the Unity3D-ARBrain venture resource organizer. Figure 4.10 underneath showcases the structure of the task resources upon the consideration of the bundle.

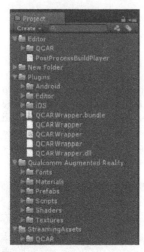

Project asset structure upon the inclusion of the
vuforia-unity-android-ios.unity package

The application's venture resources board now comprised of the accompanying supporting advancement assets portrayed beneath in light of the top level organizers.

- **Editor** - containing scripts expected to help in the dynamic association of trackable information (outline markers or picture based) inside Unity's proof-reader.
- **Plugins** - comprises of scripts in Java and local paired that guide in incorporating the product advancement pack (SDK) with android or IOS related applications.
- **Qualcomm Augmented Reality** - comprises of scripts and prefabs that guide in breathing life into AR objects.
- **Streaming Assets** - comprises of a solitary information (DAT) document containing variant points of interest.

Taking after the consideration of **Vuforia's** benefits, the outlined Brain model was then acquainted with the undertaking. The possibility of at first cutting the demonstrated parts in Maya was to make conceivable, an individual control related programming of all parts of the configuration. Another envelope titled "Cerebrum Anatomy" was made in the fundamental undertaking organizer to store the transported in model. Inside this organizer, two extra sub envelopes titled "Materials" and "Models" were additionally made. These organizers held both material surfaces and divisional cross sections that made up the model. A perspective of a portion of the substance inside the Brain Anatomy organizer after importing the model is shown in figure 4.11 beneath.

Section of project asset folder displaying split
textures and meshes of the imported brain model

4.2.3 Introducing prefabs and GameObjects to the scene

Prefabs can be depicted as resources in Unity. They are reusable items situated inside the QAR envelope of the task view board as seen beneath in figure 4.12.

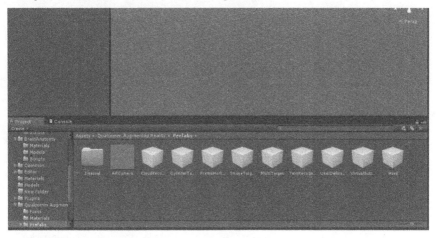

QAR folder displaying available prefabs

Various occasions of prefabs can be made and embedded into products scenes unbounded limitations. At the point when a prefab is incorporated into a scene, an example of that specific prefab is said to be made. Occurrences made, regardless of what number of, are just clones associated with the first prefab. That being said, if a modification is made on the first prefab, the change produces results over every single other occasion. Inside the prefab envelope, the **ARCamera** prefab can be found. This is an essential article required crosswise over most solidarity **vuforia** created AR applications and its motivation will be talked about further beneath.

Setting up the scene required the default primary camera on Unity to first be erased. This was supplanted with **Vuforia's ARCamera** prefab. The explanation behind the switch depends on the way that the **ARCamera's** prefab is particularly intended for AR applications. It goes about as a cell phone camera inside the scene furthermore empowers the design of properties identified with following and rendering. Keeping in mind the end goal to arrange properties, examples of the outlined model must be transported in into the scene, combined with an edge marker which model occurrences were to be anticipated on. In view of the application's planned functionalities, only one edge marker was required for its usage. The edge marker utilized was scripted at runtime on **MonoDevelop**, Unity's outsider IDE that unions the conspicuous characteristics of a content tool combined with troubleshooting highlights. All scripts made through the IDE are specifically foreign made into Unity and put away inside the Scripts envelope, noticeable on the Project Panel. The composed edge marker script can be seen beneath in figure 4.13.

```
FrameMarker0.cs

No selection

 1 MarkerTracker markerTracker = (MarkerTracker)
 2    TrackerManager.Instance.GetTracker<MarkerTracker>();
 3
 4 int markerId = 0;   // between 0 and 511
 5 string markerName = "FrameMarker" + markerId;   // unique name
 6 int markerSize = 100;   // markers are always square
 7
 8 MarkerBehaviour markerBehaviour = markerTracker.CreateMarker
 9    (markerId, markerName, markerSize);
10
11 if (markerBehaviour != null)
12 {
13    // Add a trackable event handler
14    markerBehaviour.gameObject.AddComponent<DefaultTrackableEventHandler>();
15
16    // Add an object as a child
17    GameObject brain = GameObject.AddPrimitive(PrimitiveType.BrainFull);
18    GameObject brain1 = GameObject.AddPrimitive(PrimitiveType.BrainHalf);
19
20    brain.transform.parent = markerBehaviour.transform;
21    brain1.transform.parent = markerBehaviour.transform;
22
23    brain.transform.localScale = new Vector3(0.5f, 0.5f, 0.5f);
24    brain1.transform.localScale = new Vector3(0.5f, 0.5f, 0.5f);
25
26    brain.transform.localPosition = new Vector3(0.0f, 0.25f, 0.0f);
27    brain.transform.localPosition = new Vector3(0.0f, 0.25f, 0.0f);
28 }
```

Custom marker creation and GameObject(s) assignment script

Utilizing the "**MarkerTracker**" class, a casing marker was brought into the scene and made trackable. The **MarkerTracker** class permits to make and further deal with a casing marker at runtime. Inside this class likewise lies the "**CreateMarker()**" open part work, which does the undertaking of genuine casing marker creation. Actualizing the capacity makes a casing marker with a relegated id, a name, and a separate size. As noted before in area (3.3.5) just 512 enrolled outline markers can be enlisted and followed by **Vuforia**. Hence, a made marker must be appointed an id of between 0 - 511 else, it would not be recognized by **Vuforia's** following calculation. In the script over, the edge marker made was allotted an id of 0. **GameObjects** was found in the script are vital items inside Unity, used to speak to props, landscape and characters, for example, a 3D model for this situation. The model, combined with the edge marker presented inside the script can thus be seen in the scene proof-reader. Asides the scene editorial manager see, the chain of importance board additionally shows now, the made marker and its ascribed objects in an organized configuration as found in figure 4.14.

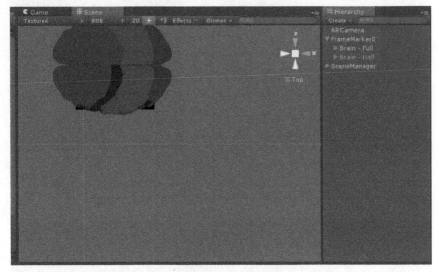

Initial views upon the creation upon marker creation and the
addition of GameObjects (lateral and medial instances of the 3D brain model).

In the figure over, the article (model) was displayed exceptionally dim inside the scene. Keeping in mind the end goal to cast a superior presentation, the "Directional Lights" **GameObject** must be presented. The procedure can be found in figure 4.15 underneath.

Addition of directional lights GameObject to light up the scene

The pith of its acquaintance was with light up both the item and scene, keeping in mind the end goal to make a brighter visual temperament as introduced in figure 4.16 underneath.

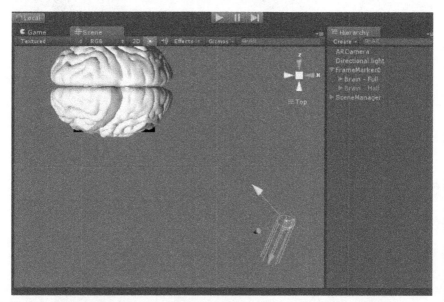

Object and Scene view upon the addition of directional light GameObject

From the picture above, it can be watched that the Directional Light **GameObject** has been put no place close to the displayed question yet at the same time plays out its capacity. This highlights the way that Directional Lights can be embedded anyplace inside the proof-reader and still affect the entire scene.

After the effective creation and reconciliation of both the edge marker and 3D model into the scene, properties of the **ARCamera** could then be conformed to fit the planned application. Highlighting the **ARCamera** from the pecking order board, introduces its modifiable properties inside the investigator board. This is found in figure 4.17 underneath.

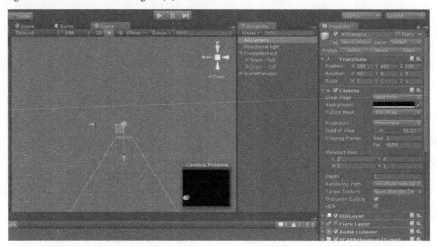

ARCamera properties displayed from the inspectors panel

One critical property of the **ARCamera** that required a change was the "close" and "far" separations of its section focuses. These settings characterize the closest and most distant separation at which an increased item will be rendered with respect to camera. The close and far separations vary per item being anticipated and their adjustment takes care of a prevalent issue known as z-battling. Z-battling happens when Unity's profundity cushion (capacity in Unity that gives the spatial mindfulness feel of **GameObjects**) confounds the separation between surfaces of a model that are exceptionally close to each other. Thus, these surfaces wind up flashing in play mode as the framework can't hand-off appropriately their draw request. Upon a few aligned projections of the model, the close property was at long last set at an estimation of 2, while the far was doled out an estimation of 5000. All different properties of the **ARCamera** were left with their default values.

Since every single required prefab and **GameObjects** had been presented and appropriately designed, programming the application's principle functionalities could then be completed.

4.2.4 Implementing the application's functionalities

Actualizing the required functionalities of the AR application required a framework called **RayCasting**. The procedure of **RayCasting** as the name suggests, includes throwing undetectable beams from a point and in a predetermined course, to distinguish climate any "Colliders" lie in the way. Colliders are segments that permit **GameObjects** to which they are joined, respond to the **RayCasting** activity. This response is accomplished through the guide of Unity's "Material science" motor (permits customized activities to be done on a gathering of articles in an underlying state). Colliders come in different shapes and sorts. They can have the primitive states of a container, a circle, or a case. Other complex examples exist for all the more sporadically formed items. On account of the mind model, being an unpredictable shape required the utilization of "Cross section Colliders". Network colliders are intended to fit the precise state of the cross sections they are doled out to. Figure 4.18 underneath delineates a cross section collider being connected to the privilege Occipital Lobe of the 3D model.

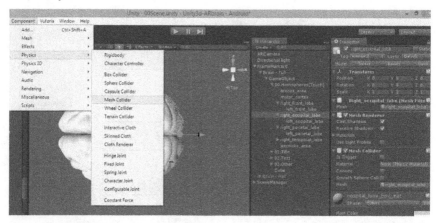

Example addition of mesh collider to a section of the GameObject

All freely transported in cross sections were appointed colliders in the same way above to give space for modified collaborations. The thought was to trigger a beam, which would be threw against any collider inside the scene through an activity (either a mouse click for standalone frameworks or direct touch for versatile interfaces). Once the beam hits a specific collider, it consequently would give data on what **GameObject** was hit. This data will be put away and can then be questioned at any occurrence to trigger an allocated usefulness.

To start programming, another script called **"RayCastDetection"** was made and appended to the primary camera (the **ARCamera).** The full and half mind cases of the model were doled out too autonomous **GameObject** variables to serve as starting focuses for the frame marker (just the full cerebrum was made obvious at beginning projection). The diverse cross section components of the full model were then put away in clusters inside the script instead of appointing them to autono- mous **GameObject** variables. This was done with a specific end goal to bunch valuable objects of the same sort as an accumulation for simpler access. Three diverse clusters were made in view of name lattices, portrayal networks and the segmented parts of the mind. The names and portrayals were likewise shrouded, just to be shown when **RayCast** activities were instantiated.

The script was made to permit the application keep running on both versatile and desktop inter- faces. Inside the script, two vital "Structures" known as the "Beam" and **"RayCastHit"** were an- nounced. Structures are an accumulation of helpful variables put away under an individual name. For this situation, both were appointed with variables names "beam" and "hit" individually. Instan- tiating the beam variable would make the imperceptible beams to be threw on individual **GameOb- jects.** While the hit variable stores data it gets when a beam hits a **GameObject** inside the scene (any part of the model). With the put away data, the application can verify the accurate point the beam hit, combined with the specific **GameObject** it hit for further allotted activities can be done. The variables were set inside a restrictive articulation, to be activated by a "for every" circle. This circle was then embedded inside a furthest beginning condition. The furthest restrictive explanation serves to confirm the stage which the application is keep running on (for this situation IOS or Android as found in figure 4.19 beneath).

```
//MOBILE DEVICES
        if ((Application.platform == RuntimePlatform.IPhonePlayer) ||
            (Application.platform == RuntimePlatform.Android)) {
```

Conditional statement to verify what platform the application is being run on before an action is carried out

The "for every" circle articulation settled inside the primary condition, is then further used to trigger the inward condition in occasions of a mouse snap or touch activity. This cooks for both desktop and cell phone settings (see figure 4.20 underneath).

```
foreach (Touch touch in Input.touches) {
        if (touch.phase == TouchPhase.Began) {
```

Loop statement to trigger internal condition upon instances of either mouse clicks or touch actions

The condition inside the circle, after building up the info technique, gives space for a beam to be threw against the **GameObject** highlighted and stores its data. This data got, then allows the "**Physics.RayCast()**" technique to be called (see figure 4.21 beneath). What this strategy does is call the material science motor and the **RayCast** technique to draw the beam in view of the position of a mouse snap or touch point on the application's interface.

```
//if left mouse button is clicked,
//create a ray that originates from the clicked position
//where we click is where we want our ray to begin
Ray ray = Camera.main.ScreenPointToRay (Input.mousePosition);
RaycastHit hit; //used to store information
//the out keyword serves as a reference for getting
//info from the hit variable
if (Physics.Raycast (ray, out hit)) {
    HitObject = hit.collider.gameObject;
```

Instantiation of ray and hit variables which serve as parameters for Physics.RayCast() method within the set condition to initialize a RayCast action.

Endless supply of any segment of the mind, two distinct arrangements of conditions were further acquainted with deal with the condition of the **GameObjects**. These conditions permitted the activity of enacting and deactivating both marks and depictions doled out to each of the displayed cerebrum areas. These depended on 4 **RayCast** projections as found in figure 4.22 underneath.

```
//Detection per each part:
if (HitObject != null) {
        if (brainElements [hitElement] == 0) {
                brainElements [hitElement] = 1;
                HitObject = null;
        } else if (brainElements [hitElement] == 1) {
                brainElements [hitElement] = 2;
                HitObject = null;
        } else if (brainElements [hitElement] == 2) {
                brainElements [hitElement] = 3;
                HitObject = null;
        } else if (brainElements [hitElement] == 3) {
                brainElements [hitElement] = 0;
                HitObject = null;
        }
}
```

If else statements used do manage detect number of times
individual GameObjects are hit by RayCast method

likewise, utilizing a "for circle" inside the activity conditions script seen underneath in figure 4.23, marks were set to be shown on first time hit by a beam, and depictions on a second hit of the same specific **GameObject**. Third and fourth hits trigger the activity of switching the perceivability of portrayals and marks.

```
//Functions per each element:
if (HitObject == null) {
        for (int x = 0; x <= brainElements.Length-1; x++) {
                if (brainElements [x] == 1) {
                        brainTitles [x].SetActive (true);
                        brainText [x].SetActive (false);
                } else if (brainElements [x] == 2) {
                        brainTitles [x].SetActive (true);
                        brainText [x].SetActive (true);
                } else if (brainElements [x] == 3) {
                        brainTitles [x].SetActive (true);
                        brainText [x].SetActive (false);
                } else if (brainElements [x] == 0) {
                        brainTitles [x].SetActive (false);
                        brainText [x].SetActive (false);
                }
                if( x >= brainElements.Length) x=0;
        }
}
```

If else statements used do control activation and deactivation of assigned labels
and description based on details of hit information retrieved

Now being developed, the application was go through the amusement renderer to confirm all activities set were responsive. The tests completed demonstrated fruitful and further coding towards the execution of interface controls were taken after on.

4.2.4.1 Assigning interface controls

Keeping in mind the end goal to accomplish pivoting, scaling and flipping between occasions of the 3D display, the **"UnityGUI"** highlight was utilized. **UnityGUI** gives space to the consistent making of essentially successful GUIs. The codes actualized produce interface controls which are instantiated, adjusted and figured out how to only one call of the **UnityGUI's "OnGUI()"** capacity.

Four controls were initially made for pivot purposes. Each were programed for left, straight up and descending style pivot of the model individually (see figure 4.24 underneath).

```
void OnGUI()
{
    //left
    if (GUI.RepeatButton (new Rect (0, Screen.height / 2-(150 * widthHeightRatio)/2,
        100 * widthHeightRatio, 150 * widthHeightRatio), "")) {
        halfBrain.transform.Rotate(Vector3.down * 4);
        fullBrain.transform.Rotate(Vector3.down * 4);
    }
    //right
    if (GUI.RepeatButton (new Rect (Screen.width-(100 * widthHeightRatio),
        Screen.height / 2-(150 * widthHeightRatio)/2, 100 * widthHeightRatio,
        150 * widthHeightRatio), "")) {
        halfBrain.transform.Rotate(Vector3.up * 4);
        fullBrain.transform.Rotate(Vector3.up * 4);
    }

    //up
    if (GUI.RepeatButton (new Rect (Screen.width/2-(125 * widthHeightRatio),
        0, 250 * widthHeightRatio, 100 * widthHeightRatio), "")) {
        halfBrain.transform.Rotate(Vector3.right * 4);
        fullBrain.transform.Rotate(Vector3.right * 4);
    }
    //down
    if (GUI.RepeatButton (new Rect (Screen.width/2-(125 * widthHeightRatio),
        Screen.height-(100 * widthHeightRatio), 250 * widthHeightRatio,
        100 * widthHeightRatio), "")) {
        halfBrain.transform.Rotate(Vector3.left * 4);
        fullBrain.transform.Rotate(Vector3.left * 4);
    }
```

AR interface control script to enable rotation of lateral and medial sections of the 3D model

Taking after the expansion of this rationale, flipping functionalities to permit exchanging amongst full and half occurrences of the 3D cerebrum model were then actualized through the code bit found in figure 4.25 underneath.

```
//1
if (GUI.Button (new Rect (0, 0, 240 * widthHeightRatio,
    80 * widthHeightRatio), "Brain")) {
    halfBrain.SetActive(false);
    fullBrain.SetActive(true);
}
//2
if (GUI.Button (new Rect (0, 80 * widthHeightRatio +10,
    240 * widthHeightRatio, 80 * widthHeightRatio), "Half-Brain")) {
    halfBrain.SetActive(true);
    fullBrain.SetActive(false);
}
```

AR interface control script to enable toggling between lateral and medial sections of the 3D brain model

In conclusion, the scrap showed in figure 4.26 underneath was executed to initiate the model's scaling highlights. All arranged control execution assignments were formally fulfilled now.

```
//-
if (GUI.RepeatButton (new Rect (Screen.width-(240*widthHeightRatio),
    0, 120 * widthHeightRatio, 120 * widthHeightRatio), "-")) {
    i-=0.4f;
    fullBrain.transform.localScale = new Vector3(8+i, 8+i, 8+i);
    halfBrain.transform.localScale = new Vector3(8+i, 8+i, 8+i);

}
//+
if (GUI.RepeatButton (new Rect (Screen.width-(120*widthHeightRatio),
    0, 120 * widthHeightRatio, 120 * widthHeightRatio), "+")) {
    i+=0.4f;
    fullBrain.transform.localScale = new Vector3(8+i, 8+i, 8+i);
    halfBrain.transform.localScale = new Vector3(8+i, 8+i, 8+i);

}
```

AR interface control script to enable scaling of lateral and medial sections of the 3D brain model

4.2.4.2 Code implementation considerations

The, "**widthHeightRatio**" variable relegated in each of the control codes was actualized for screen determination administration purposes. It was doled out to get a decent determination proportion for the GUIs on each showcase screen which the application was to be executed. That is, the GUIs will naturally acclimate to superbly fit any screen they are shown on. The controls were intended to look semi-straightforward on the screen and are adjusted near the edges of the interface; regardless of any gadget the application is keep running on. This style of configuration was considered to abstain from deterring the clients' perspective of the interface environment, while collaborating with the application. Another basic structure found in the executed control codes is the "Vector3". Its motivation was to permit going around 3D headings and positions in virtual space for exact scaling and turn activities.

Asides the above related components, the "**GUI.RepeatButton**" and "**GUI.Button**", are another arrangement of critical structures utilized as a part of various occurrences of the control codes. It ought to be noticed that both structures don't work in the same way, independent of their close comparative titles. The essential distinction between their capacities is identified with the way that the **GUI.RepeatButton** will give back a Boolean estimation of valid, the length of the specific control is persistently squeezed. This would permit its allotted activity to be done uncertainly till the control is discharged. The **GUI.Button** structure then again, just permits an activity to be submitted once, independent of a persistent hang on the control. Mulling over this, both occurrences inside the code were deliberately executed. On account of flipping between model occasions (full or half mind), the **GUI.Button** was utilized. Regardless of to what extent the controls to flip the full or half mind models are held down, the client would not see a physical reaction to the activity the length of it has as of now been embedded once. Its planned capacity required a solitary example activity. Thusly, using the **GUI.RepeatButton** to bring about a monotonous conferring of the activity on squeezing the control, would have appeared to be unreasonable. With respect to revolution and scaling cases be that as it may, the **GUI.RepeatButton** was the ideal decision. This is attributable to the reality such responsibilities are most appropriate as control press nonstop activities. Controlling these specific capacities would be very badly arranged assignments, if the clients needed to constantly tap the controls at interims keeping in mind the end goal to deliver visual reactions of the activity. Figure 4.27 underneath portrays arrangement positions of all made GUI catches on the last application's interface.

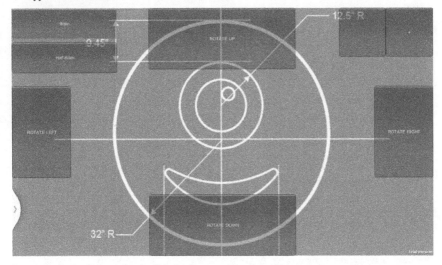

Preview of application splash screen interface displaying placement positions of controls

After sparing the application's script document, a last test was completed to ensure every single appointed control worked as required. The tests demonstrated effective and the application was presently prepared to be sent for assessment.

CHAPTER 5: METHODOLOGY

The study as prior expressed means to weigh exactly what amount executing AR in a tertiary level instruction setting, can powerfully affect and enhance understudy learning. This has been accomplished by examining its execution as opposed to customary strategies for instructing, while likewise mulling over, client acknowledgment and powerful inspiration levels got from utilization of the innovation. Consequently, the present part serves to transfer the decision of approach that was connected in the study, factual related techniques for information examination, instrument plans and information accumulation strategies. Likewise, the populace and test determination technique, combined with the test setup and strategies have additionally been exhibited.

This study was guided by two examination questions: (1) Can Learning encouraged by AR improve understudy getting a handle on force? (2) Does AR based learning grow the capacity to focus and engagement of understudies? (3) Can AR be acknowledged as a feasible coaching apparatus inside tertiary Institutions?

Taking into account the primary question, the specialist has conjectured that the utilization of AR ought to mirror a critical increment in learning improvements, contrasted with conventional learning strategies. With an end goal to give a response to the second and third inquiries be that as it may, the specialist has additionally played out a diagnostic appraisal of understudies' inspiration and acknowledgment levels, in connection to the utilization of the innovation.

5.1 Research Design

The exploration was completed exploiting two survey plans. These were utilized to assemble quantitative related information from the study members after the examination. A quantitative technique for methodology was led the study since it gave space for measurable investigation of the aggregated information. Likewise, attributable to the way of the study (Experimental) and the expected number of members, observatory and individual style meetings would not have given the level of information honesty exhibited using the unknown polls.

Furthermore, being a test research, both an autonomous and a needy variable were required. This required member to be part into Experimental and Controlled gatherings separately. The trial bunch got the opportunity to work with the ARBrain application while the controlled gathering was given customary 2D print materials through the activity. The strategy for direction was in this manner allotted as the free variable while taking in increases got from post-test assessments of members served as the needy variable. A t-Test for Independent Samples was used to test the speculation in light of information assembled upon post-test assessments. The explanation behind the decision depended on the built up reality that parametric related tests, for example, the t-test, have turned out to be significantly more adaptable in examining information (**Brown and Melamed, 1990;** Williams, 1996; Keppel and **Wickens, 2004).** Upon the fruitful gathering of results, number-crunching method for the reliant variable at last were looked at between both Experimental and Controlled gatherings, taking into account the expressed estimations of the pronounced autonomous variable.

As a major aspect of the study, it was likewise imperative to set up the level of motivational impact the ARBrain application had on exploratory gathering. Innovation acknowledgment as characterized by **Louho, Kallioja and Oittinen (2006)** is the way by which individuals acknowledge, receive and see the utilization of innovation. Throughout the years, models that serve to gauge the number of clients get the opportunity to acknowledge or use specific advancements have been recommended and executed. The Technology Acceptance Model (TAM) (Davis, 1989), Innovation Diffusion Theory (**Rogers, 1995**) and the Unified Theory of Acceptance and Use of Technology (**Venkatesh et al., 2003**) were noted from examination as three of such models. Of the three said, TAM was picked as the favoured instrument to set up the expressed target. This was inferable from the way that it was seen to be the most tentatively accepted and generally used in data framework considers (Lederer et al., 2000; King and He, 2006). While Lederer et al. (2000) have enlisted more than 15 effectively distributed studies utilizing the TAM model through a 10-year time frame (1989-1999), King and He (2006) have likewise called attention to 88 effectively investigated productions in view of the model. The model was created, exploiting the planned conviction, demeanour and conduct model proposed by **Ajzen and Fishbein (1980)** to upgrade the prescient capacity of their Theory of Reasoned Action. **Davis (1989)** recommended that pivotal determinants which affected the intention to use any innovation can be foreseen through saw handiness and usability. Cap since its creation, has been adjusted in various connections and tried on various advancements. **Davis (1989, p.985)** expressed that its objective is "to give a clarification of the determinants of PC acknowledgment that is for the most part fit for clarifying client conduct over a wide scope of end-client processing innovations and client populaces, while in the meantime being both niggardly and hypothetically supported". Figure 5.1 beneath portrays the TAM plan as proposed by **Davis (1993).**

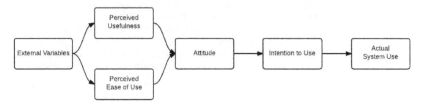

Original TAM design by Fred Davis. Adapted from Davis (1993)

Attributable to the way that client acknowledgment concentrates on shift per specific advancements being examined, scientists much of the time consolidate the primary TAM outline with other characterized develops considered material to the particular assessed innovation (Legris, Ingham and Collerette, 2003). Choosing the decision of builds to set up client acknowledgment of frameworks has turned into a critical range of examination in the Information Systems field (Chesney, 2006). The term builds allude to weight related components that guide in breaking down the utilization and acknowledgment of the innovation. Table 5.1 beneath presents case of past studies which have executed the TAM outline with included broadened builds.

Examples of Past studies which chose to extend TAM to suit the particular technologies under analysis

Other Academic Like minds	Extended Constructive involvement
Online Gaming (Hu and Lu, 2004)	Critical Mass, Flow, Social
Programmed LEGO designed Robot (Chesney, 2006)	Delight Users (DU)
Email Alert Interface Systems (Serenko, 2008)	Users ease of usage (UEOU)
Gaming in Classrooms (Bourgonjon, Valcke, Soetaert & Schellens, 2009)	Learning Opportunities, Delighted Gaming feelings, Sex

In connection of this study, the level of happiness was considered as an essential variable that could affect learners' utilization of the innovation. Throughout the years, this has turned into a typical quality utilized in client acknowledgment research (Chesney, 2006; Serenko, 2008). Past examination from Davis (1989) additionally highlighted saw helpfulness and Ease of Use as similarly imperative variables towards a beneficial outcome on learner inspiration and innovation acknowledgment. He built up that when clients discover an innovation simple to utilize and trust it will enhance their learning, they similarly accordingly expect to encourage receive it later on. Thinking about the variables highlighted, the table 5.2 underneath presentations the picked builds that were utilized to set up the last survey plan for assessment.

Constructive involvement	Set
Delight Users (DU)	The level to which an action helped out using a specific innovation is esteemed pleasant (Chesney, 2006). This measures the client's sentiment delight and determined through communicating with the application. (Interior Stimuli)
Users ease of usage (UEOU)	The level to which clients of the framework feel its utilization will be sans exertion (Davis, 1989). (Outside Stimuli)
System usability (SU)	The level to which clients feel that using the innovation will help in improving their assignment achievements (Davis, 1989). (Interior Stimuli - Satisfaction)
Aesthesis users (AU)	The level to which clients have formulated cognizant expectations to use or not use certain particular future practices (Davis, 1989).

Information accumulated from the Technology Acceptance request setup was examined utilizing factual relapse examination as a part of request to build up connections between the develops and give a response to the related inquiry.

5.2 Instruments design

5.2.1 Multi-choice questionnaire

The survey comprised of 15 specific reaction questions identifying with the human mind life structures material to be investigated by both gatherings of members. It was made to serve as a post-test strategy for examination towards the estimation of learning additions. Owing the substantial number of members selected for the study, it demonstrated the best technique for assessment as finished returns could be quickly scored. Every inquiry was appointed a sum of four choices, comprising of only one right reply amongst the decisions advertised. The poll upon its creation was surveyed by a teacher in brain science at the Middlesex University Mauritius Branch Campus with a specific end goal to measure the legitimacy of the inquiries. Upon audit, certain progressions were required. These were completed and brought about the last plan.

5.2.2 Technology acknowledgment poll

Identifying with innovation acknowledgment, the specialist accumulated a survey made up of 18 things to measure the level of motivational impact accomplished using the ARBrain application. The outlined survey was comprised of 4 develops as prior handed-off in segment 5.1. The things in each of the builds were weighed in view of a 5-point composed Likert scale as takes after: 1 = Strongly Disagree, 2 = Disagree, 3 = Neutral, 4 = Agree, 5 = Strongly Agree. Things drafted to weigh Perceived Enjoyment were received from the innovation acknowledgment instrument plan displayed by Chesney (2006). The rest of the things of the other 3 develops then again, were embraced from the first TAM model by Davis (1989), which from various reports had been entrenched and accepted.

5.3 Study members

A sum of 80 members were enrolled to participate in this study. This comprised of a blend of understudies from an assortment of offices at Middlesex University Mauritius Branch Campus. The understudies were specifically drawn nearer and the examination was promoted as "A Study to analyse the utilization of an option learning apparatus in classroom settings". Likewise, the members in the early stages, were not educated on the kind of learning materials they would work with till they had been part into test and controlled gatherings individually. That being said, they were all however asked for to bring along their cell phones, with a favoured accentuation on tablets if inside their ownership. It was important to minimize the measure of data went on to the understudies now, in order to keep up an unprejudiced spotlight on the examination. Understudies enrolled before the day set out for the analysis, upon their consent to agree to the study, were given further points of interest by method for electronic mail. The points of interest gave related particularly to the title of the study, the time and the area where the trial was to be held. Then again, members selected upon the arrival of the examination, attributable to the bustling scholarly session plans, must be educated verbally about every single essential point of interest before being drafted in.

5.4 Ethical considerations

As indicated by Blackstone (1975), research including human members by and large requests a variety of target populaces, few of which might be defenceless or do not have a complete fitness to give endorsement. Remembering this, moral rules must be mulled over before the study was led as it clearly includes human interest. A brief subtle element of the trial was henceforth submitted to the Middlesex University morals board of trustees for audit and a formal endorsement. This was important keeping in mind the end goal to verify that the investigation was not the slightest bit going to bring about any dangers at all to the members.

5.5 AR and conventional guideline treatments

The materials used in the study were created with the guide of print-based and web assets (Parker, 2003; Gamon and Bragdon, 1998; Brainwaves.com, 2014; Macmillan.org.uk, 2014). Endless supply of materials for both the AR and conventional medicines, its substance was reviewed by teachers in Psychology at the University. The last outlined variants included literary related data, combined with 2D or 3D representations (contingent upon the treatment) delineating the distinctive parts of the mind and their related capacities.

The AR direction treatment included physical custom markers relegated to every member. Through the technique, members of the test gathering were told to use the markers as a manual for give knowledge to the outlined subject substance. Every marker was to display a 3D model of the human mind on top of them, giving the members the chance to control and investigate them. Then again, printed instructional materials were allotted to members of the controlled gathering for assessment. It ought to be noted now that both substance were precisely similar, with the main separating element being the 3D models in the AR guideline materials and 2D pictures in the customary direction materials.

5.6 Procedure

As an aftereffect of the bustling scholarly session, it was for all intents and purposes difficult to accumulate each of the 80 members with a specific end goal to do the study in one day. Henceforth, the activity must be spread out through a 2day period in view of members' accessibility. The scientist through arranging time and availabilities was likewise ready to partition the members in an equivalent 40:40 proportion. The outlined test was led in 3 stages which went on for a 3-hour time frame on both days. Members, upon their landing in the venue, were given a pocket containing 40 collapsed post-it notes. Engraved on each of the notes in an equivalent 20 split proportion, had the terms ARI and TI. ARI alluding to Augmented Reality Instruction and TI, customary direction. Members, through this implies, were then allocated to either trial or controlled gatherings, in view of the subtle elements on every post-it take note of that was drawn. When they were all settled in their separate gatherings, a letter of acquaintance was given out with every member, separating the planned objectives and targets of the analysis. Upon the effective initial breakdown, they were then given agree structures to round out, perceiving their acknowledgment to share in the analysis.

In the second stage, both trial and controlled gatherings were then guided through their separate treatment techniques. With respect to the AR instructional treatment, the specialist reasoned that tablet gadgets would be the best decision for presentation. In any case, attributable to the way that not all subjects of the ARI relegated bunch had entry to this, the treatment must be led in clusters. The analyst could accumulate a sum of 10 tablet gadgets and thus required that the exploratory gathering be part into sub gatherings of 10 members each. Prior to the initiation of the activity, the ARBrain application was introduced on all the accessible tablet gadgets. Members appointed to the ARI bunch needed to experience a brief session before the activity, keeping in mind the end goal to hand-off right utilization of the custom AR markers in accordance with the application. It additionally cleared some other misguided judgments the members had. After gathering together, the session, they were then permitted to make utilization of the application. The TI related members in any case, did not require an instructional meeting, neither did they require to be part for their treatment. They were given their guideline materials, instantly upon the short acquaintance and their concurrence with share in the analysis through the assent marking strategy.

The last period of the activity required the members of both ARI and TI gatherings to round out the post-test multi-decision survey intended to measure learning picks up. The ARI treatment bunch moreover, likewise needed to round out the Technology Acceptance planned poll to measure engagement and motivational levels. Figure 5.2 underneath portrays a diagrammatic representation of the systems brought out through the ARBrain assessment process.

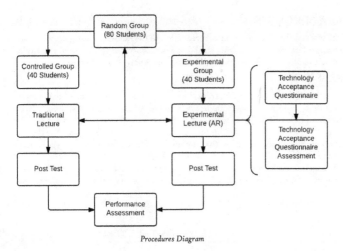

Procedures Diagram

Once the activity was finished, every one of the members were all around refreshing and a full question was given. They were additionally given contact subtle elements of the specialist, in the event that they required more data in connection to the study.

CHAPTER 6: ANALYSIS

This section points of interest the discoveries uncovered through the factual investigation of quantitative information assembled from the members. It has been separated into two areas as takes after: (1) Post Test Analysis Results (2) Technology Acceptance Analysis and Results.

6.1 Post-test analysis results

Keeping in mind the end goal to examine results from the post test questions exhibited to the members, a two followed t-Test for autonomous examples was conveyed utilizing the Microsoft Excel 2013 information examination highlight. This was to identify if both gatherings played out any distinctively on the tests. To start, an invalid and option speculation were characterized. For this situation, the analyst began off with the suspicion that the method for results from both exploratory and controlled gatherings are equivalent (Ho: μExp = μCont). This served as the invalid speculation. The option theory then again, was characterized to identify if the method for results got from trial and controlled gatherings were any diverse (H1: μExp ≠ μCont). The outcomes can be found in table 6.1 beneath.

t-Test: Paired Two Sample for Means obtained with
a set Significance Level of 0.05 and a 95% Confidence Interval.

	ARI Post Test	TI Post Test
Number of scores collected	N	392
Mean	12.7	10
Variance	2.01025641	5.128205128
Observations	40	40
Degree of freedom (df)	39	
t Stat	5.746381986	
P-Value (T<=t) two-tail	1.16553E-06	
t Critical two-tail	2.02269092	

The likelihood esteem (P-Value) alludes to the likelihood of the study result happening, under the assumed thought that the pronounced invalid theory is valid (Coolidge, 2006). With a specific end goal to help the specialist figure out if to dismiss the invalid theory or not, a noteworthiness level of 0.05 was set as a check esteem in the framework. Essentially, the target in theory approval is to confirm if the p-esteem acquired is not as much as, equivalent to, or more noteworthy than the characterized centrality level (Shi and Tao, 2008). In situations where it is not exactly the doled out hugeness level (i.e. 0.05), it would mean there is an under 5% percent risk that the outcomes from both gatherings are equivalent. Then again, if the p-worth is equivalent to the centrality level or more noteworthy, it highlights the way that there is no critical contrast between the outcomes from both the gatherings. The two-tail t Critical worth, likewise exhibits the t esteem that should be surpassed all together for the contrast between means got to be regarded huge, in light of the doled out 5% hugeness level.

In light of the table results above, with a subsequent P-Value of 0.00000016553, route not exactly the set criticalness estimation of 0.05, the invalid theory expressed was thus dismisses by the analyst. Additionally, the t esteem got from the information with a relegated level of flexibility of 39 (t (39)), was 5.746381986. This gave the analyst a second motivation to dismiss the invalid speculation as it surpasses the characterized two tail t basic quality. Therefore, the outcomes (t(39)= 5.746381986; p= of 0.00000016553) clarify why the ARI subjects were connected with altogether higher mean scores than the TI subjects. Figure 6.1 underneath showcases a graphical portrayal of the contrast between means got from both gatherings at a 95% certainty interim.

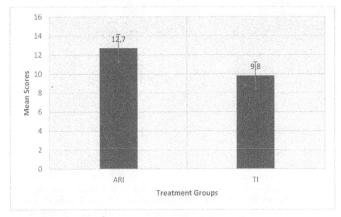

Graph depicting difference between mean scores derived from both ARI and Tertiary institutions

6.2 Technology acceptance analysis and results

6.2.1 Constructive reliability

With an end goal to accept the unwavering quality of the builds used inside the embraced TAM survey, the analyst completed an underlying pilot study comprising of 15 members. These members were additionally selected from a blend of divisions inside the University yet had no immediate contribution in the primary study. They did however experience the ARI treatment exercise before giving their input through the finish of the inferred poll. The information investigation was accomplished using the SPSS windows-based information info and examination program. Cronbach's alphas were connected so as to set up the dependability of the determined 18 things, four builds survey, as showed underneath in table 6.2.

Level of Construct reliability

Set Constructive involvement	Number of related imputes	Obtained Cronbach's alpha values
Delight Users (DU)	6	0.876
Users ease of usage (UEOU)	4	0.814
System usability (SU)	4	0.779
Aesthesis users (AU)	4	0.891

Cronbach's alpha serves as an inward consistency measure that decide how shut an arrangement of characterized things is connected as a gathering. The outcomes introduced in the table above demonstrated great levels of unwavering quality amongst the builds. This was in contrast with the well-known acknowledged inward consistency rules exhibited in the table beneath (Koning and Franses, 2003):

Cronbach's alpha values	Degree of Internal consistency
$\alpha \geq 0.9$	Excellent
$0.7 \leq \alpha < 0.9$	Good
$0.6 \leq \alpha < 0.7$	Acceptable
$0.5 \leq \alpha < 0.6$	Poor
$\alpha < 0.5$	Not acceptable

6.2.2 Delight Users (DU) imputes results

Results from the examination of things of this develop can be found in table 6.4 underneath. Taking into account the outcome, everything except 3 of the members uncovered through their reactions that using the ARBrain application was enjoyable. A 95% lion's share of the members taking into account the scale, either emphatically concurred or consented to the idea that the ARBrain application was lovely. As far as the amount they appreciated utilizing the application, everything except 1 of the members either firmly concurred or concurred. Independent of the way that 70% of the members were not upbeat upon the finish of the activity, the staying 30% were impassive. Taking into account eagerness to rehash the experience, 92% of the members indicated interest, 5% were detached and 3% oppose this idea. What's more, a 96% dominant part likewise either emphatically concurred or consented to the idea that utilizing the ARBrain application as a learning apparatus, gave a fascinating knowledge.

PE item results (1 = Strongly Disagree, 2 = Disagree, 3 = Neutral, 4 = Agree, 5 = Strongly Agree; N = 40)

	Imputes	Strongly Disagree	Disagree	Neutral	Agree	Strongly Agree	Mean ($\bar{x}$)	Std. Dev. (S)
1	Fun to use.	0.0%	0.0%	4.9%	42.1%	53.0%	3.39	0.487
2	A complete Device.	0.0%	0.0%	7.3%	54.7%	40.0%	3.31	0.491
3	Enjoyability.	0.0%	0.0%	1.5%	46.0%	54.5%	3.53	0.446
4	Unsatisfied using the device.	0.0%	0.0%	30.3%	49.6%	20.1%	2.73	0.491
5	Continuous user experience.	0.0%	2.7%	4.9%	45.3%	47.1%	3.34	0.573
6	Satisfied using the device	0.0%	0.0%	3.7%	32.4%	63.9%	3.56	0.466

6.2.3 Users ease of usage (UEOU) imputes results

Results from the analysis of items of this construct can be seen in table 6.5 below. The results show that a majority of participants strongly agreed or agreed that learning to use the ARBrain application was easy. Regarding the item asking if they found it easy to navigate and manipulate all functions of the ARBrain application, all but 5 of the participants were in agreement. Eighty-two percent were also in agreement that it was easy getting used to the ARBrain application, while 20% were indifferent. Nonetheless, a 91% majority positively concluded that the ARBrain application was ease to utilize.

	Imputes	Strongly Disagree	Disagree	Neutral	Agree	Strongly Agree	Mean (x̄)	Std. Dev. (S)
1	"UserAlfas", The device is self-explainable to use	0.0%	0.0%	3.2%	59.9%	36.9%	3.34	0.425
2	"UserBetas", It's easy to manipulate all navigation parts of the ARBrain.	0.0%	0.0%	7.8%	46.9%	45.3%	3.31	0.515
3	"UserARgo", It's easy to adapt to the ARBrain devices.	0.0%	0.0%	20.2%	36.9	44.9%	3.24	0.658
4	Overall "UserTouch" found the ARBrain devices user friendly	0.0%	0.0%	9.1%	56.8%	34.1%	3.17	0.515

6.2.4 System usability (SU) imputes results

Results from the investigation of things of this develop can be found in table 6.6 underneath. As indicated by the discoveries, 93% of the members were in assention that the ARBrain application empowered them comprehend ideas identifying with the human cerebrum life structures. Every one of the members likewise emphatically concurred or concurred with the idea that the ARBrain application could improve their comprehension of the functions and procedures of the human cerebrum. With respects if AR advances would make it their studies simpler, everything except one member either unequivocally concurred or concurred that it would.

	Imputes	Strongly Disagree	Disagree	Neutral	Agree	Strongly Agree	Mean (x̄)	Std. Dev. (S)
1	Using ARBrain devices will ensure "UserAlfas" to understand the brain anatomy quickly.	0.0%	0.0%	6.6%	49.1%	44.3%	3.36	0.502
2	Using ARBrain devices will support "UserBetas" to understand the functionality; processes of the brain.	0.0%	0.0%	0.0%	49.0%	51.0%	3.49	0.414
3	AR mechanism will ensure user friendly ability to manipulate applications "UserARgo".	0.0%	0.0%	1.8%	42.2%	56.0%	3.54	0.441
4	"UserTouch" find AR Devices useful in acquiring knowledge.	0.0%	0.0%	1.4%	39.5	59.1%	3.58	0.423

6.2.5 Aesthesis users (AU) imputes results

Results from the investigation of things of this develop can be found in table 6.6 underneath. In summation, all reactions in respects the aim to utilize AR innovations were sure. Almost every one of the respondents emphatically concurred or consented to utilize any framework ascribed to AR innovation when it got to be accessible at the University and executed in their commonplace branches of knowledge. Eighty-percent of them recommended from reactions that they the innovation as often as possible on the off chance that they had entry it while 13% were uninterested. Regardless, if gave access to AR advancements, everything except 2 members meant their expectation to exploit it.

ITU item results (1 = Strongly Disagree, 2 = Disagree, 3 = Neutral, 4 = Agree, 5 = Strongly Agree; N = 40)

	Imputes	Strongly Disagree	Dis- agree	Neu- tral	Agree	Strongly Agree	Mean (x̄)	Std. Dev. (S)
1	I prefer to use any device attributed to AR mechanism when it becomes available in my areas of academic institution.	0.0%	0.0%	6.6%	49.1%	44.3%	3.36	0.502
2	I prefer to use other softwares like the ARBrain in other learning environment.	0.0%	0.0%	0.0%	49.0%	51.0%	3.49	0.414
3	Haven had the access to the device, I would often use this device.	0.0%	0.0%	1.8%	42.2%	56.0%	3.54	0.441
4	Supposing I am opportune to a new system, I intend to use it.	0.0%	0.0%	1.4%	39.5	59.1%	3.58	0.423

A spellbinding investigation in connection to the 4 builds is shown in Table 6.7 beneath. All in all, all members emphatically reacted to tolerating AR innovation (with got implies above 3.0 from 4 and little deviation values). They saw the actualized innovation generally speaking as pleasant, simple to utilize, and beneficially helpful. They additionally communicated a status to utilize the innovation if and when executed later on.

Construct descriptive analysis
(1 = Strongly Disagree, 2 = Disagree, 3 = Neutral, 4 = Agree, 5 = Strongly Agree; N = 40)

Set Constructive	Mean (x̄)	Std. Dev. (S)
PE	3.394	0.576
PEOU	3.374	0.630
PU	3.584	0.532
ITU	3.538	0.611

With an end goal to decide the effects of PE, PEOU and PU on ITU, the specialist completed a relapse investigation. Aftereffects of the examination demonstrated that PE and PEOU had no critical effect on members' aim to utilize AR ($p=.344$, $p=.091$ separately). Then again, PU was observed to be critical towards deciding ITU (transcendent impact result taking into account ANOVA: $F_{(1, 38)} = 51.085$, $p<0.05$)). An autonomous t-test investigation likewise uncovered a solid relationship existing between the reliant variable ITU and free variable PU ($r=0.75$). A R_2 estimation of 0.563 acquired served to demonstrate that about 65% of changes in ITU were as an aftereffect of equivalent changes in members' PU. Alternate variables from their qualities, still demonstrated no proof of an effect on ITU (PE ($r=0.83$); PEOU($r=0.433$). Likewise, PE and PEOU exhibited co-linearity resilience aftereffects of 0.274 and 0.433. As a consequence of the way that the qualities surpasses 0.10, it demonstrates the information had no co-linearity issues.

CHAPTER 7: DISCUSSION

The point of the study was to measure the impacts of an AR instructional treatment to the customary conventional method of educating on tertiary level understudies in today's society. To accomplish this, an AR application (ARBrain) was created to help understudies in better comprehension ideas identifying with the human mind life systems. The application was worked with the plan to break down the outcomes acquired from its usage. This was with an end goal to give answers to 3 set up examination questions: (1) Can learning encouraged by AR upgrade understudy getting a handle on force? (2) Does AR based learning grow the ability to focus and engagement of understudies? (3) Can AR be acknowledged as a suitable coaching instrument inside tertiary Institutions? A received arrangement of volunteer inspecting including 80 members from a blended scope of divisions and no past encounters with AR innovation, was utilized as a part of this study. In a similarly split proportion, the members were separated into both an Augmented Reality Instruction (ARI) bunch and a Traditional Instruction (TI) bunch. Contingent upon the relegated bunches, members were either treated to Augmented Reality based directions or Traditional 2D guidelines.

Through measurable results got from an autonomous t-test investigation of post-test scores, a solid huge contrast in learning increases was found. Members from the ARI bunch exhibited much preferred results over the individuals who shared in the TI treatment. This gives a response to first research question and furthermore, underpins the specialist's underlying expressed speculation. The outcomes encourage reinforce the conviction that AR as an instructional device, emphatically can change understudies' apparent perspective of spatial ideas. It consequently bolsters the consequences of studies found through the underlying audit of literary works (Duenser and Hornecker, 2007; Dunleavy, Dede, and Mitchell, 2008; Klopfer and Squire, 2008; Chang, Morreale and Medicherla, 2010).

In connection to discoveries recovered from investigation of the Technology Acceptance test on the ARI bunch, results proposed that members saw the AR application as charming, and with practically no exertion, simple to utilize. Furthermore, members were likewise persuaded that AR as a learning device, can be exceptionally helpful towards upgrading their instructive execution. As per Sullo (2009), inward and outside related jolt inferred through learning, add to the level of inspiration or demotivation understudies' gain. In this manner, the positive levels of saw usability (outside boosts), delight (inside jolts) and convenience (inner boosts) give a built up motivation to the distinction in execution between the ARI and TI bunches. This likewise introduces a response to second research question postured.

Finally, towards setting up if the innovation will be acknowledged inside tertiary organizations, further examination was completed on the develops by method for measurable relapse. Of the considerable number of builds, there was a decidedly solid relationship between saw helpfulness and members' aim to utilize. The other two develops in examination, displayed sensibly noteworthy connections towards aim to utilize. This outcome corresponds with the discoveries of Davis (1989) as it backings the rationale that the length of clients discovers the framework valuable, they will in all probability develop on their behavioral inspirations towards embracing the innovation. The analyst in any case, additionally trusts that there are informative motivations to the absence of similarly persuading importance regarding saw pleasure and usability on expectation to utilize.

7.1 Study limitations

In connection to satisfaction, the analyst feels the incorporation of more intelligent elements, for example, the expansion of sound prompts and haptic signals could have started up the pleasure levels in members. Likewise, considering the reality none of the members had come in contact or ever utilized an AR related innovation, this legitimately clarifies the inadequate qualities in connection to its apparent usability. It took the members a short session to see how the application functioned and actually does not propose they had gotten to be specialists in its utilization. In spite of the fact that the outcomes were adequate to give a response to both the second and third research address, the specialist trusts the above clarifications prompted the primary restriction of the study. On the off chance that more elements were actualized and additional time was allotted to the convenience session, there is a probability that the connections between saw satisfaction and value on expectation to utilize could have been more positive.

Another impediment to the study was in admiration to the way that the assessment was just done at one tertiary organization. Organizing with different Universities inside the time period set out for the task was not a practical plausibility and thus prompt the analyst's decision. As a consequence of this, it is difficult to figure out whether the discoveries for the most part represent itself with no issue without more information from a lot of Universities in Mauritius.

CHAPTER 8: CONCLUSION AND FUTURE WORK

This study explored the impacts of an AR instructional treatment to the normal customary method of educating on tertiary level understudies in today's society. The outcomes demonstrated that AR as a learning device can improve understudy learning, as well as expansion their inspiration and drive to learn. The outcomes likewise propose the usage of the innovation inside tertiary foundations will be promptly received by understudies the length of its demonstrated helpfulness is built up. AR in today's tertiary class settings, can serve as an intense and productive device in empowering understudies' associate with complex spatial wonders. The control of 3D items introduces the required data important to build up associations taking into account how these complex spatial marvels work. By acquainting AR with classrooms, it is the analyst's conviction that there could be certain advantages in accordance with the nature obviously educational modules introduced in life systems as well as in all controls. Sooner rather than later, an augmented exploration could be led with a specific end goal to reach to a more extensive scope of Universities. This would be valuable towards setting up a more grounded pertinence to the outcomes at present acquired. Likewise, it would be a smart thought to rehash the study utilizing an option lesson content. Independent of the way that the specific lesson actualized turned out well, it is helpful to legitimize that AR can truly adjust to different lesson substance in tertiary training settings.

REFERENCES

1. Arvanitis, T., Petrou, A., Knight, J., Savas, S., Sotiriou, S., Gargalakos, M. and Gialouri, E. (2007). Human factors and qualitative pedagogical evaluation of a mobile augmented reality system for science education used by learners with physical disabilities. *Pers Ubiquit Comput*, 13(3), pp.243-250.
2. Arvanitis, T., Williams, D., Knight, J., Baber, C., Gargalakos, M., Sotiriou, S. and Bogner, F. (2011). A Human Factors Study of Technology Acceptance of a Prototype Mobile Augmented Reality System for Science Education. *adv sci lett*, 4(11), pp.3342-3352.
3. Azuma, R. (1997). Survey of Augmented Reality. Presence: Teleoperators and Virtual Environments, 6 (4), pp.355-385.
4. Azuma, R., Baillot, Y., Behringer, R., Feiner, S., Julier, S., MacIntyre, B. (2001). Recent advances in augmented reality. *Computers & Graphics*, pp.1-15.
5. Behzadan, A., and Kamat, V. (2012). A Framework for Utilizing Context-Aware Augmented Reality Visualization in Engineering Education. *12th International Conference on Construction Application of Virtual Reality*, pp.5-8.
6. Bellotti, F., Berta, R., De Gloria, A. and Margarone, M. (2005). Implementing tour guides for travelers. *Hum. Factors Man.*, 15(4), pp.461-476.
7. Behringer, R., Jun, P., Sundareswaran, V. (2002). Model-based visual tracking for outdoor augmented reality applications. *Proceedings of International Symposium on Mixed and Augmented Reality*, pp.277-322.
8. Billinghurst, M., Kato, H., and Poupyrev, I. (2001). The magicbook-moving seamlessly between reality and virtuality. *Computer Graphics and Applications, IEEE*, 21(3), pp.6-8.
9. Birk, J. (1996). Dynamic Visualization in Chemistry. *J. Chem. Educ.*, 73(6), p.526.
10. Blackstone, W. (1975). The American Psychological Association Code of Ethics for Research Involving Human Participants: An Appraisal. *The Southern journal of philosophy*, 13(4), pp.407--418.
11. Blake, M. and Butcher-Green, J. (2009). Agent-customized training for human learning performance enhancement. *Computers & Education*, 53(3), pp.966-976.
12. Bloxham, J. (2014). Augmented Reality Learning. *ITNOW*, 56(3), pp.44-45.
13. Botden, S. and Jakimowicz, J. (2008). What is going on in augmented reality simulation in laparoscopic surgery?. *Surg Endosc*, 23(8), pp.1693-1700.
14. Brainwaves.com, (2014). The Brain - Diagram and Explanation. [online] Available at: http://brainwaves.com [Accessed 10 Mar. 2014].
15. Brown, S. and Melamed, L. (1990). *Experimental design and analysis*. Newbury Park, Calif.: Sage Publications.
16. Brush, T. and Saye, J. (2004). Supporting learners in technology-enhanced student-centred learning environments. *International Journal of Learning Technology*, 1(2), p.191.
17. Cassan, A. (2006). *The brain*. Philadelphia: Chelsea House.
18. Champion, E. (2006). Enhancing Learning through 3D Virtual Environments. In E.K. Sorenson, and D.O. Murchu (Eds.), *Enhancing Learning through Technology*. pp.103-124.
19. Chang, G., Morreale, P., and Medicherla, P. (2010). Applications of augmented reality systems in education. *In Society for Information Technology & Teacher Education International Conference*, pp.1380-1385.
20. Chaurasia, S. (n.d.). Augmented Reality in Retail: A Revolutionary Next Generation Technology. *SSRN Journal*.
21. Chen, C. and Tsai, Y. (2012). Interactive augmented reality system for enhancing library instruction in elementary schools. *Computers & Education*, 59(2), pp.638-652.
22. Cheng, K. and Tsai, C. (2012). Affordances of Augmented Reality in Science Learning: Suggestions for Future Research. *Journal of Science Education and Technology*, 22(4), pp.449-462.
23. Choi, J. and Kim, G. (2012). Usability of one-handed interaction methods for handheld projection-based augmented reality. *Pers Ubiquit Comput*, 17(2), pp.399-409.

24. Chuang, Y. (2014). Increasing Learning Motivation and Student Engagement through the Technology- Supported Learning Environment. *CE*, 05(23), pp.1969-1978.
25. Coolidge, F. (2006). *Statistics*. Thousand Oaks, Calif.: Sage Publications.
26. D., C., E., A. and D., E. (2012). Enhancing the Tourism Experience through Mobile Augmented Reality: Challenges and Prospects. *International Journal of Engineering Business Management*, p.1.
27. Datta, P. (2010). A preliminary study of ecommerce adoption in developing countries. *Information Systems Journal*, 21(1), pp.3-32.
28. Dey, A. and Sandor, C. (2014). Lessons learned: Evaluating visualizations for occluded objects in handheld augmented reality. *International Journal of Human-Computer Studies*, 72(10-11), pp.704-716.
29. Display devices. (1993). *Displays*, 14(3), p.188.
30. Drummond, T. (2011). *High Speed Matching and Tracking Slides*. [online] Available at: https://www.qualcomm.com/media/documents/files/qualcomm-research-lecture-high-speed-matching-and-tracking-slides.pdf [Accessed 29 Aug. 2014].
31. Dünser, A. and Hornecker, E. (2007). An Observational Study of Children Interacting With an Augmented Story Book. *Technologies for E-Learning and Digital Entertainment, Springer Berlin Heidelberg*, pp.305-315.
32. Dunleavy, M., Dede, C. and Mitchell, R. (2008). Affordances and Limitations of Immersive Participatory Augmented Reality Simulations for Teaching and Learning. *Journal of Science Education and Technology*, 18(1), pp.7-22.
33. El Sayed, N., Zayed, H. and Sharawy, M. (2011). ARSC: Augmented reality student card. *Computers & Education*, 56(4), pp.1045-1061.
34. Gamon, D. and Bragdon, A. (1998). Building mental muscle. 1st ed. Cape Cod, MA: Brainwaves Books.

35. Gilbert, S., Blessing, S. and Blankenship, L. (2009). The accidental tutor: overlaying an intelligent tutor on an existing user interface. pp.4603--4608.

36. Gizmag, (2014). *IKEA Mobile AR Catalog Application*. [image] Available at: http://www.gizmag.com/ikea-augmented-reality-catalog-app/28703/ [Accessed 28 August 2014].
37. Hawkes, D. (1999). The Perception of Visual Information. *"Virtual Reality and Augmented Reality in Medicine", the Perception of Visual Information*, pp.361-390.
38. Hicks, J.D., Flanagan, R.A., Petrov, P.V., Stoyen, A.D. (2002). Eyekon: augmented reality for battlefield soldiers. *Proceedings. 27th Annual NASA Goddard/IEEE Software Engineering Workshop*, pp.156-163.
39. Hillman, T. (2013). Finding space for student innovative practices with technology in the classroom. *Learning, Media and Technology*, 39(2), pp.169-183.
40. HITLab, (n.d.). ARToolkit algorithm driven tracking scenario. [image] Available at: http://www.hitl.washington.edu/artoolkit/documentation/userarwork.htm [Accessed 13 Jul. 2014].
41. Hua, H., Girardot, A., Gao, C. and Rolland, J. (2000). Engineering of Head-Mounted Projective Displays. *Applied Optics*, 39(22), p.3814.
42. Justi, R. and Gilbert, J. (2002). Models and Modeling in Chemistry Education. *(J.K. Gilbert, O.D. Jong, R. Justi, D.F. Treagust & J.H. Van Driel, Eds.) Chemistry education: Towards research-based practice*. MA: Kluwer Academic Publishers.
43. Kaufmann, H., Schmalstieg, D. and Wgner, M. (2000). A Virtual Reality Application for Mathematics and Geometry Education. *Education and Information Technologies*, 5(4), pp.263-276.
44. Kaufmann, H. (2002). Construct3D: an augmented reality application for mathematics and geometry education. *Proceedings of the tenth ACM international conference on Multimedia (MULTIMEDIA '02)*.
45. Kaufmann, H. and Schmalstieg, D. (2003). Mathematics and Geometry Education with Collaborative Augmented Reality. *Computers & Graphics*, 27(3), pp.339-345.

46. Kaufmann, H., Steinbugl, K., Dunser, A., and Gluck, J. (2005). General training of spatial abilities by geometry education in augmented reality. *Cyberpsychology & Behavior*, 8(4), pp.330.

47. Kaufmann, H. (2009). Dynamic differential geometry in education. *Journal for Geometry and Graphics*, 13(2), pp.131-144.

48. Keppel, G. and Wickens, T. (2004). *Design and analysis*. Upper Saddle River, N.J.: Pearson Prentice Hall.

49. Klopfer, E. and Dede, C. (2008). Handheld Augmented Reality Project (HARP) & Alien Contact! Unit Overview.pp.1-3. Available at: http://isites.harvard.edu/icb/icb.do?keyword=harp&pageid=icb.page69619 [Accessed 5 Sep. 2014].

50. Koning, A. and Franses, P. (2003). *Confidence intervals for Cronbach's coefficient alpha values*. Rotterdam: Erasmus Research Institute of Management (ERIM).

51. Kuznetsov, A. and Kuznetsova, O. (2011). Looking for Ways to Increase Student Motivation: Internationalisation and Value Innovation. *Higher Education Quarterly*, 65(4), pp.353-367.

52. Langlotz, T., Grubert, J. and Grasset, R. (2013). Augmented reality browsers. *Commun. ACM*, 56(11), pp.34-36.

53. Laparoscopic cholecystectomy. (1991). *BMJ*, 302(6776), pp.593-594.

54. Lee, K. (2012). Augmented Reality in Education and Training. *TechTrends*, 56(2), pp.13-21.

55. Louho, R., Kallioja, M. and Oittinen, P. (2006). Factors affecting the use of hybrid media applications. *Graphic Arts in Finland*, 35(3), pp.11-21.

56. Luursema, J., Verwey, W., Kommers, P., Geelkerken, R., & Vos, H. (2006). Optimizing conditions for computer assisted anatomical learning. Interacting with Computers, 18(5), pp.1123-1138.

57. Macmillan.org.uk, (2014). The brain - structure and function - Cancer Information - Macmillan Cancer Support. [online] Available at: http://www.macmillan.org.uk/Cancerinformation/Cancertypes/Brain/Aboutbraintumours/Thebrain.aspx [Accessed 9 Mar. 2014].

58. Members, A. (2014). *ACCU :: Writing Extendable Software*. [online] Accu.org. Available at: http://accu.org/index.php/journals/402 [Accessed 23 Aug. 2014].

59. Johnson, L., Levine, A., Smith, R., and Stone, S. (2011). The 2011 Horizon Report. Austin, Texas: The New Media Consortium.

60. Kalkofen, D., Mendez, E., and Schmalstieg D. (2007). Interactive Focus and Context Visualization in Augmented Reality. *Proc. 6th IEEE International Symposium on Mixed Reality (ISMAR '07)*, pp.191-200.

61. Karvounidis, T., Chimos, K., Bersimis, S. and Douligeris, C. (2014). Evaluating Web 2.0 technologies in higher education using students' perceptions and performance. *Journal of Computer Assisted Learning*, 30(6), pp.577-596.

62. Klopfer, E. and Squire, K. (2007). Environmental Detectives—the development of an augmented reality platform for environmental simulations. *Education Tech Research Dev*, 56(2), pp.203-228.

63. Kroeker, K. L. (2010). Mainstreaming augmented reality. *Communications of the ACM*, 53(7), pp.19-21.

64. Kurzweil Accelerating Intelligence. (2014). Military-Grade Augmented Reality. [image online] Available at: http://www.kurzweilai.net/military-grade-augmented-reality-could-redefine-modern-warfare [Accessed: 28 August 2014].

65. Layar, (2009). *Products | Layar App | Layar*. [online] Available at: https://www.layar.com/products/app/ [Accessed 01 Sep. 2014].

66. Li, C. (2006). Augmented Reality in Medicine. *Proceedings of Advanced Interface Design*, pp. 49-52.

67. Martin, K., Galentino, R. and Townsend, L. (2014). Community College Student Success: The Role of Motivation and Self-Empowerment. *Community College Review*, 42(3), pp.221-241.

68. Martín-Gutiérrez, J., García-Domínguez, M., Roca-González, C., Sanjuán-HernanPérez, A. and Mato-Carrodeguas, C. (2013). Comparative Analysis between Training Tools in Spatial Skills for Engineering Graphics Students based in Virtual Reality, Augmented Reality and PDF3D Technologies. *Procedia Computer Science*, 25, pp.360-363.
69. McCartney, M. (2013). Motivation + Skill = Success. *Science*, 340(6133), pp.661-661.
70. Milgram, P. and Kishino, F. (1994). A Taxonomy of Mixed Reality Visual Displays. IEICE Transactions on Information Systems, E77-D (12).
71. Nicholson, D. (2013). Augmented reality grows up. *Engineering & Technology*, 8(4), pp.32-35.
72. Nicolau, S., Soler, L., Mutter, D. and Marescaux, J. (2011). Augmented reality in laparoscopic surgical oncology. *Surgical Oncology*, 20(3), pp.189-201.
73. O'Rourke, M. (1998). *Principles of three-dimensional computer animation*. New York: Norton.
74. Pachoulakis, I. (2012). Augmented Reality Platforms for Virtual Fitting Rooms. *The International journal of Multimedia & Its Applications*, 4(4), pp.35-46.
75. Parker, S. (2003). Brain. 1st ed. Chicago, Ill.: Heinemann Library.
76. Presselite, (n.d.). *The London Tube Mobile AR Navigation App*. [image] Available at: http://www.presselite.com/iphone/londontube/ [Accessed 01 Sep. 2014].
77. Qualcomm, (2014). *Qualcomm® Vuforia™ Home*. [online] Available at: http://www.qualcomm.com/solutions/augmented-reality [Accessed 26 Aug. 2014].
78. Shi, N. and Tao, J. (2008). *Statistical hypothesis testing*. Singapore: World Scientific Pub.
79. Shibata, T. (2002). Head mounted display. *Displays*, 23(1-2), pp.57-64.
80. Spreer, P. and Kallweit, K. (2014). Augmented Reality in Retail: Assessing the Acceptance and Potential for Multimedia Product Presentation at the PoS. *MR*, 1(1), pp.23-31.
81. Strijbos, J. (2011). Assessment of (Computer-Supported) Collaborative Learning. *IEEE Trans. Learning Technol.*, 4(1), pp.59-73.
82. Sullo, R. (2009). *The motivated student*. Alexandria, Va.: Association for Supervision and Curriculum Development.
83. Sunday Morning Herald, (2011). *Zugara's Virtual Dressing Room technology for Online Stores*. [image] Available at: http://www.smh.com.au/technology/technology-news/another-blow-to-retailers-virtual-dressing-rooms-20110809-1ijxa.html [Accessed 28 August 2014].
84. The Application of Augmented Reality in Education Compared to Virtual Reality. (2013). *AISS*, 5(8), pp.620-627.
85. Vera-Portocarrero, L. (2007). Brain facts. New York: Chelsea House.
86. Wang, J., Xiao, X., Hua, H. and Javidi, B. (2014). Augmented Reality 3D Displays with Micro Integral Imaging. *Journal of Display Technology*, pp.1-1.
87. Wikitude, (2009). *App - Wikitude*. [online] Available at: http://www.wikitude.com/app/ [Accessed 01 Sep. 2014].
88. Williams, J. (1996). *Statistical methods*. Lanham, Md.: University Press of America.
89. Wu, H., Lee, S., Chang, H. and Liang, J. (2013). Current status, opportunities and challenges of augmented reality in education. *Computers & Education*, 62, pp.41-49.
90. Yovcheva, Z., Buhalis, D., Gatzidis, C. and van Elzakker, C. (2014). Empirical Evaluation of Smartphone Augmented Reality Browsers in an Urban Tourism Destination Context. *International Journal of Mobile Human Computer Interaction*, 6(2), pp.10-31.
91. Zhu, C., Liang, X., Kockro, R. and Serra, L. (2004). Accuracy evaluation of an augmented reality enhanced surgical navigation system. *International Congress Series*, 1268, p.1329.

YOUR KNOWLEDGE HAS VALUE

- We will publish your bachelor's and master's thesis, essays and papers

- Your own eBook and book - sold worldwide in all relevant shops

- Earn money with each sale

Upload your text at www.GRIN.com and publish for free